YES, IT'S A JUNGLE OUT THERE

Taxable and tax-free money market funds . . . corporate, U.S. government, and municipal bond funds . . . load and no-load funds . . . income funds . . . growth funds . . . income *and* growth funds . . . conservative funds . . . aggressive funds . . . international funds . . . global funds . . . high cap funds . . . low cap funds . . . high-tech funds . . . no-tech funds . . . one fund after another . . . hundreds of funds . . . thousands of funds . . . with new funds all the time . . . all with ads aglow with promises and prospectuses filled with dense print and daunting numbers.

FORTUNATELY, YOU DON'T HAVE TO BE LOST IN IT

Not when you have the user-friendly guide you can instantly turn to and follow with confidence for your whole investment life—

THE NEATEST LITTLE GUIDE TO MUTUAL FUND INVESTING

JASON KELLY is a young technical writer for a computer company in Silicon Valley. His job is to take difficult and boring technical information and reduce it to a simple form that is readable and maybe even enjoyable. He lives in Los Angeles.

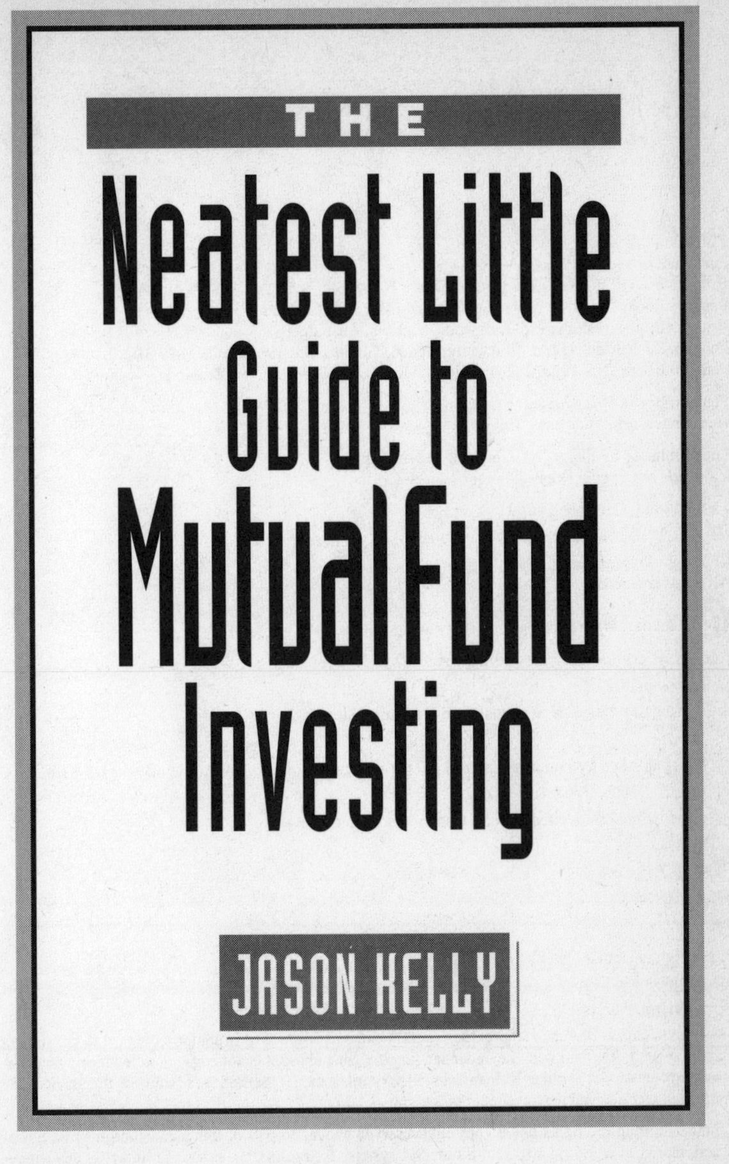

THE Neatest Little Guide to Mutual Fund Investing

JASON KELLY

A PLUME BOOK

PLUME
Published by the Penguin Group
Penguin Books USA Inc., 375 Hudson Street, New York, New York 10014, U.S.A.
Penguin Books Ltd, 27 Wrights Lane, London W8 5TZ, England
Penguin Books Australia Ltd, Ringwood, Victoria, Australia
Penguin Books Canada Ltd, 10 Alcorn Avenue, Toronto, Ontario, Canada M4V 3B2
Penguin Books (N.Z.) Ltd, 182–190 Wairau Road, Auckland 10, New Zealand

Penguin Books Ltd, Registered Offices:
Harmondsworth, Middlesex, England

First published by Plume, an imprint of Dutton Signet,
a division of Penguin Books USA Inc.

First Printing, December, 1996
10 9 8 7 6 5 4 3 2 1

LIBRARY OF CONGRESS CATALOGING-IN-PUBLICATION DATA:

Kelly, Jason.

The neatest little guide to mutual fund investing / Jason Kelly.

p. cm.

"First published by Plume, an imprint of Dutton Signet, a division of Penguin Books USA Inc."

ISBN 0-452-27709-4

1. Mutual Funds—United States—Handbooks, manuals, etc.

I. Title.

HG4930.K45 1996

332.63'27—dc20

96-25162

CIP

Printed in the United States of America
Set in Times Roman

PUBLISHERS NOTE

This publication is designed to provide accurate and authoritative information in regard to the subject matter covered. It is sold with the understanding that the publisher is not engaged in rendering financial or other professional service. If financial advice or other expert assistance is required, the service of a competent professional person should be sought.

Ten Steps to Investing in Mutual Funds

Reader:

For definitions of key terms, see the Glossary on pages 130–31.

Contents

1 The Best Investments You Can Buy

Welcome aboard! This easy guidebook teaches everything you need to know to begin an investment program in mutual funds. This chapter explains what a mutual fund is and then discusses why funds are so good.

What Is a Mutual Fund?

Mutual funds have become the choice of millions of investors across the world. Today you can select from over 8,000 funds—far more selections than you'll find on the New York Stock Exchange. Americans have poured billions of dollars into mutual funds recently for goals like retirement, vacations, new homes, improvements on old homes, cars, business expenses, and higher education. In fact, one in four Americans invests in mutual funds, and the value of all mutual funds combined is greater than the nation's bank deposits. So what is a mutual fund?

A mutual fund is a gathering of money from investors with a common objective. The "mutual" part is the common objective, and the "fund" part is the money. When you invest in a mutual fund, you put your money in a pot with other people's money. The fund manager uses all of it to buy stocks, bonds, and money market instruments. In exchange for your money you're given shares in the fund.

Investors with a Common Objective

A share's price fluctuates with the value of what the fund owns. So if you send $100 to a fund whose shares are worth $10, you'll own ten shares. If the value of the stocks, bonds, or money market instruments that the fund owns increases, the price of the shares increases and so does your investment. Say, for example, that the price of each share rises to $11. Your initial $100 will have turned into $110 because each of your ten shares is worth a dollar more. Of course, it works in the other direction too. But more on that later.

The Price of Each Fund Share Is Its Net Asset Value, or NAV

The price of each fund share is called its "net asset value," or NAV. At the end of every day, the NAV is determined by dividing the value of a fund's investments by the number of shares sold. For example, if a fund owns $20 million worth of stocks, bonds, or money market instruments and investors hold 5 million shares of the fund, then the fund's NAV is $4. The fund arrives at $4 after dividing $20 million by 5 million.

Since the number of shares you own is proportionate to the amount you invest, your $100 returns the same percentage of profit or loss as a pension fund's $10 million. For example, if you place $100 in a fund that achieves a 10 percent annual return, your account will be worth $110 at the end of the year. A pension fund with $10 million in the same fund will have $11 million at the end of the year. Both you and the pension fund added 10 percent to your account's worth even though the pension fund invested a lot more money. That's the magic of mutual funds.

Open-end vs. Closed-end Funds

The most common funds are called *open-end* funds. This is the type I've been discussing so far. Whenever somebody sends money to an open-end fund, they purchase shares in the fund that are worth that day's NAV, plus a sales commission if there is one (more on that in the next section). An investor can sell shares back to the fund for the current NAV at any time.

The other kind of mutual fund is *closed-end.* Closed-end funds sell a limited number of shares. If you want to buy shares in one of these funds, you need to buy them on the stock market from somebody who already owns them. They are listed on the stock exchange just like company stocks and bonds. They also fluctuate in price and are worth what people are willing to pay for them—which might be more or less than their NAV's. The selling price of closed-end funds is not based solely on the value of the stocks, bonds, or money market instruments that they own.

This guidebook shows how to invest in open-end mutual funds. They are much more prevalent and easily accessible to everyone.

Load vs. No-load Funds

Among the thousands of open-end funds some charge a sales commission, called a *load*, on the money you invest. This can be as high as 8.5 percent of what you send in, which is a lot. For instance, if you send $100 to a load fund that charges 8.5 percent it immediately takes out $8.50 for itself and only invests $91.50 for you.

Beware of Loads

The remaining funds do not charge this load and are appropriately called *no-load* funds. These terms are muddied because some technically no-load funds charge other fees that aren't sales commissions. Luckily, the other fees and commissions are easily identified, and you'll learn how in this guidebook.

Some people assume that load funds charge a commission because they are better managed than no-loads. This hasn't proven to be the case, however. No-load funds have done as well as or better than load funds, particularly if you factor in losses from the commission. Remember that in a fund charging an 8.5 percent load, only $91.50 of every $100 is actually invested.

Does that mean that you'll get your money back once the fund posts an 8.5 percent gain? No. The commission was taken off the top of your principal amount, $100, which means you have less money working for you. The 8.5 percent of $100 is equal to $8.50 but against your invested amount of $91.50 it's only worth $7.78. The fund actually needs to return 9.3 percent in order to fully pay back the commission you paid. Not good.

No-load funds are a better choice. Why begin your investment at a disadvantage? A no-load fund insures that all of your money goes to work for you right away and that any returns instantly increase the value of your investment. You don't have any commissions to recoup.

Why Mutual Funds Are So Good

Mutual funds are good investments for a number of reasons. For starters, they allow beginners to place their money in the same expert hands as the big guys. Corporate pension dollars aren't given any better treatment in a mutual fund than the scraped-together savings of a high school student.

It's convenient to invest in a fund too. With postage-paid envelopes, a busy woman can write a check to the fund of her choice and have it on its way before she begins the day's errands. Or she can use a toll-free phone number to call the fund and have money transferred directly from her bank account. There's no waiting in lines to invest in a mutual fund.

Mutual Funds Are Convenient

Mutual funds are an easy way for small-timers to diversify their investments. It wouldn't be wise to risk all of your money on a single stock, hoping that it pays off. Without mutual funds, people with little money to invest would have few choices because they couldn't afford to own a bunch of different investments. They'd be forced to put their money in a bank savings account or CD, where the returns are usually lower. In a fund, however, every dollar sent in is spread across many different investments, sometimes even international ones. That way if a single investment does poorly, the rest can keep the losses to a minimum. Mutual funds can earn more money than bank accounts but are safer than owning individual stocks.

Some investments tie your money up for long periods of time. You can't easily get at the money you've put into a house or withdraw from a CD before it matures. Mutual funds are liquid, meaning that investors can get their money out at any time. Some funds even offer check writing and debit cards. You should note, however, that being able to get your money easily doesn't mean that it's always wise to do so. Most mutual funds fluctuate in value and require time to smooth out the fluctuations. You'll learn more about time horizons and your specific investment goals in the next chapter.

Finally, the United States Securities and Exchange Commission (SEC) watches over the mutual fund industry to make sure things remain fair. While this can't guarantee big winnings, it's comforting to know that there are rules in this game.

Aristotle wrote about a business venture of the Greek philosopher Thales, all of whose writings are lost. Skeptics ridiculed Thales, saying that his supposed wisdom left him penniless. Surely, they advanced, if he was as wise as he claimed, he would be wealthy. Thales finally reacted by purchasing every olive press in Miletus during a year when his study of meteorology forecasted a record crop of olives. Since his presses were the only available, Thales charged outrageous prices and amassed a fortune from the single growing season. After tallying his wealth and making the sum known, he sold every press back to the community and resumed his position as philosopher.

2 Preparing to Invest

With mutual funds, as with everything else, there are certain things everybody should understand. You need to know how to steer before you can drive on the freeway, know how to say "whoa!" before you enter a rodeo, and know about the relationship between time and risk before you invest in mutual funds.

This chapter gives you the necessary background you need to begin planning your mutual fund investment program.

Choose Your Goals

Goals are the name of the game for investing. Nothing else matters until you know why it is that you're willing to part with money from your daily life to buy something that brings you no amount of pleasure. An investment's only value lies in what it is able to eventually buy for you. In and of itself it has no worth.

That means you have to know what it should eventually be able to buy for you, and when. You'll need a different strategy for your first house payment than you will for your first date. They'll probably occur at different times too, unless you're a slow mover.

Goals Matter More Than Age

Investment books are notorious for recommending that young people invest aggressively, middle-age people invest moderately, and older people invest safely. This is too simplistic. The thing that really matters is the specific goal, not the age of the person working toward the goal.

The rationale in many investment books is that young people have a greater tolerance for risk than older people because they have the rest of their lives to make up for lost money. And, the thinking goes, old people don't have as much time and might be depending on their investments for immediate needs. All of this is true if the person in question, young or old, has only one investment and the goal of that investment is retirement.

Goals Are the Name of the Game

The real factor to consider when evaluating investments is not the age of the investor, but the time frame of the goal. It is true that a twenty-year-old should place his retirement account in a more aggressive fund than a fifty-year-old's retirement account. The reason is that the twenty-year-old has a much longer time between now and his retirement than the fifty-year-old.

However, what if the twenty-year-old is putting money away for a world tour that he wants to take when he's twenty-five? Now it doesn't matter that he's only twenty. The goal will be won or lost in a period of five years. The young man needs to treat his world tour goal differently than he treats his retirement. Likewise, if the fifty-year-old sets money aside for his granddaughter's graduation in ten years, he should treat that goal differently than he treats his retirement. The fifty-year-old's granddaughter account should be invested more aggressively than the twenty-year-old's travel account because it has a longer time horizon: ten years instead of only five years.

The point of this discussion is to show you how important it is to define specific goals for your investments. Don't rely on your age to indicate how to invest your money. It's your goals that matter.

Make Your Goals Specific and Exhilarating

In addition to being specific, it's good to make your goals exhilarating. Setting money aside for an exciting purpose is easier than denying yourself a shopping spree so you can save for a rainy day. Don't get me wrong. Rainy days should be prepared for, but make sure that some of your investment money goes toward a goal that is exhilarating and motivates you to invest. Placed in the right context, even saving for a rainy day can be exhilarating.

Instead of saying that you want to "be financially comfortable" or "have a lot of money," say that you want to have $100,000 within ten years. Start adding tangible possessions to your goals like "a three-bedroom ski lodge in Aspen." Eventually you will have a vision for yourself that is made up of many different goals: "I want to own a Lexus Sport Coupe, live in my cabin in Aspen, and have $100,000 invested by 1999." Now you're talking.

Goals Should Be Exhilarating!

Set goals that are important to you. They don't need to be extravagant, but they should motivate you, and they should be specific so that you can measure your progress toward reaching them. Maybe having $1,000 invested by New Year's and a dress for your daughter on her birthday are more your style.

Here's an excerpt from a worksheet that helps you define your goals. I've provided an example of one of my goals, owning a Lexus Sport Coupe, in addition to the common goal of college funding:

What You Want	What It Will Cost	When You Want It Measured in Years	Annual Payment Cost Divided by Years	Monthly Payment Annual Payment Divided by 12
Lexus Sport Coupe	$45,000	5	$9,000	$750
College Funding	$40,000	10	$4,000	$333

At the back of this guidebook you'll find the full worksheet that you can photocopy and use for your goals. Fill it in as you read along. Note that not all goals are as easy to price as a Lexus Sport Coupe. College funding, for example, depends on a number of variables. Will your child attend a community college or Stanford? Perhaps he or she will be getting financial aid and scholarships to ease the burden. Be aware that this worksheet isn't comprehensive enough for retirement planning. Retirement is a unique goal, and you need to consider factors such as inflation and your expected investment return. You'll read all about retirement on page 115, and even see where to order free kits to help you plan a retirement investment program.

The Three Basic Fund Objectives

There are three basic mutual fund objectives. They are growth, income, and stability. Every fund strives to achieve some combination of the three. Some funds focus exclusively on one objective, others concentrate on one objective while devoting a portion of their money to the remaining two, and still others mix the three objectives evenly. Growth, income, and stability are like the three primary colors. They can combine to create any desired variation.

All Investors Juggle the Three Objectives

Each of the three objectives focuses on one of three asset classes. The asset classes are stocks, bonds, and the money market. There is a risk with any investment that it will lose money, and the three asset classes have varying degrees of risk associated with them. Long periods of time make any investment less risky because it has a chance to recover from losses. For short periods of time, stocks present a high risk of losing money, bonds present a medium risk, and the money market presents a low risk. You'll read a complete discussion of risk, beginning on page 12.

Funds are sometimes categorized by their asset classes. For example, a magazine might list all the stock funds together, the bond funds together, and the money market funds together. I find this somewhat misleading. The true connection between the funds being listed together is not their main asset class, but the objective being pursued by investing in that asset class. The assets themselves are just tools to achieve the objective.

To better understand the relationship between the three objectives and their asset classes, think about baking a loaf of bread. When you set out to bake a loaf of bread and a friend asks what you are doing, you don't say that you're using the oven. You say that you're baking a load of bread. The oven helps you bake the bread, but using the oven is not your prime concern. It's true that you won't be using the cupboard to bake the bread, but the oven is still just the tool you're using. In fact, the cupboard does have a function in baking the bread; it holds the flour and yeast. But your objective is to bake the bread, and your main tool is the oven.

So it is with mutual funds. Each objective has a main tool—its main asset class—but other asset classes might play a part in achieving the objective. Since mutual funds can combine asset classes, listing funds under a heading of one asset class (such as "Bond Funds") implies that the fund invests only in that particular class. The truth is that the funds might invest in all three classes with a preference given to bonds. If so, then it is correct to identify the fund as having an income objective. The one exception to this is with funds seeking pure stability. They always invest exclusively in the money market.

Each objective is appropriate for different goals. Depending on what investors hope to accomplish with their money, they choose funds with different objectives. A description of each objective follows.

Growth

The growth objective wants to increase the value of an investor's principal. That is, if you send $100 at the beginning of the year, you would like it to turn into $110, $120, or $150 by the end of the year.

Growth is usually accomplished through the purchase of stock that appreciates over time. The idea with growth is precisely what flea-market dealers seek: to buy low and sell high.

You'll learn more about specific kinds of growth funds on page 37.

Income

The income objective wants to maintain a flow of cash from an investor's principal. So if you send $100 at the beginning of the year, you would expect to receive payments during the year or possibly at the end of the year. You could use the cash to purchase items or you could invest it. At the end of the year your principal would probably not have become as large as it would have under a growth objective, but you would have enjoyed a stream of income.

Income is generally accomplished by either purchasing stocks that pay dividends or by purchasing bonds.

You'll learn more about specific kinds of income funds on page 40.

Stability

The stability objective wants to keep your principal from shrinking. It isn't concerned with getting you rich or providing you with steady income; it just wants to protect the money you already have. So if you send $100 at the beginning of the year, you would expect it to be there in full at the end of the year.

Stability is accomplished by purchasing reliable investments from the money market like U.S. government bonds. Even if the whole investment world crumbles around you, Uncle Sam will honor his obligations.

Since the only way to guarantee stability is by investing entirely in the money market, funds that have stability as their only objective are usually referred to as money market funds. You won't find them listed under the heading "Stability." You'll learn more about money market funds on page 46.

Summary

Here is a summary of each fund objective, its main asset class, and the risk that your investment will lose money in the short term:

Fund Objective	Invests Mainly In	Risk
Growth	Stocks	High
Income	Bonds	Medium
Stability	Money Market	Low

Risky Business

Every investment involves risk.

Even Fishing Can Be Risky

Even if you rubber-band your money into rolls of $100 bills and stash it in a tire swing, you're not safe. You might forget which tire swing you hid it in. The rubber band could crack and let your money drift away on the wind, one bill at a time. What if some kid finds it and reads this guidebook and invests it all in mutual funds? He might retire before you do.

Mutual funds carry risk too. The amount is different for every fund category, which makes it easy to find funds that match your tolerance for risk. You might be a person who doesn't mind a daily price fluctuation. There are others who burst a vessel every time the market dips five points.

Risk and Reward

The more risk you take, the greater your potential reward. If an investment is so safe that it will take a war to lose money on it, then it won't pay as much as the one that is a long shot. It's just like betting at the horse races. You might lose everything on a long shot, but if it comes through you'll be rolling in money.

With mutual funds risk can be reduced to a science. By looking at the year-by-year returns and volatility of various funds and noting their investment objective, you can be sure that your money is going to a place that balances the right amount of risk against the rewards you expect to reap.

There are two flavors of risk with investing. The first is what everyone is aware of: that their money will shrink or disappear altogether. In investor's lingo, this is called a capital loss. People immediately think of this danger when they hear the word "risk." Scenarios for this range from owning stock in a company that goes bankrupt to having Cousin Wally skip town with the money he borrowed from you.

There Goes Cousin Wally

However, there's a different flavor of risk that can do as much damage. It's the risk that your money won't be worth what it should be over time. As you know, inflation drives prices steadily upward every year. If prices rise at 3 percent a year and your money is only earning 2 percent, then you're losing 1 percent of your money's purchasing power each year. Is that a safe investment?

Sometimes it looks like it. If you put $100 into a bank account that earns 2 percent a year interest, at the end of your first year you would have $102 in the account. It doesn't look like you lost money because your $100 is still there and has earned $2 more. But because of the 3 percent inflation cost, it takes $103 to buy what only $100 would have bought a year ago. And even with your interest payment, you have only $102, which means that your money buys less than it did a year before. Overall, you are $1 behind. Actually, you're even further behind because you must pay taxes on the $2 interest.

Your investments should be risky enough to earn the amount of money needed for their goals during the time available to reach those goals. The key is time, which is what I'll discuss next.

Time and Risk* Are Your Friends

Risk isn't a bad thing. It's something to be aware of and incorporate into your investment strategy, but not something to

*I use the term "risk" to mean day-to-day risk unless otherwise specified. So when you see "risk," you know I'm referring to the risk that your money will shrink or that its value will rise and fall in short time periods.

be afraid of. More risk brings more reward with time. A solid rule is that the more time you have to invest, the riskier your investments should be.

Not Much Time to Invest for This

That's an easy concept to understand. If your goal is to buy your husband a new pair of shoes for Christmas and he has expensive taste, you might start saving in July. Let's say the shoes cost $500.

It wouldn't be wise to choose a risky fund to store the money until December. The investment market goes through peaks and valleys, and your six-month time frame could fall into one of the valleys. Your shoe fund might be worth half what you paid for it by Christmas.

Instead you should choose a money market fund because stability is its objective. Money market funds are managed to protect your money, and you might just be able to afford a pair of socks with those shoes from the interest you earn.

On the other hand, if you decide your husband can go barefoot for all you care and that the $500 would be better spent toward your retirement in twenty years, risk becomes your friend. You don't need that money for a long time, and it doesn't matter to you what it's worth next month. In twenty years, since the market tends to rise, your $500 could become a small fortune. Do you care what it was worth ten years ago once you retire? Not really. As long as its general movement was upward and it reached your goals, you're happy.

Don't Worry, His Feet Will Be Happy on the Beaches of Retirement

If you chose the Christmas shoes money market fund for your retirement, you wouldn't have as much to retire on. It's true that at any given point along the path to retirement, your principle investment would have been preserved, but in the end you would have less money.

For example, let's say you place $100 into a high-risk fund with growth as its objective and $100 into a low-risk fund with stability as its objective. Three months later, the high-risk $100 has shrunk to $90 while the low-risk $100 has grown to $102.

One year later the high-risk $100 is worth $95 while the low-risk $100 is worth $105. So far, the evidence suggests that the low-risk fund is the better choice. That's usually true for the short-term.

Over the long-term, however, the story changes. At the twenty-year mark, your risky $100 is worth $700 and the low-risk $100 is only worth $300. See how it works? Over short time periods, the low-risk fund is protected from shrinking but only increases a tiny bit in value. In those same time periods, high-risk money might shrink or grow so that it is worth more or less than its original value. Over time, though, the high-risk fund should surpass the low-risk by a big margin.

Remember that there are two types of risk. What I've been discussing in the previous example when I write "risky" is the risk that the value of your investment will shrink. Given a long time frame, "risky" means something else. It means there's a possibility that your money will not be worth the amount needed to achieve your goals. Funds that are risky in one way tend not to be risky in the other. For example, if a fund is risky in the sense that your money might be worth a different amount from day to day, it is probably not risky over long periods of time. On the other hand, a very stable fund that won't let the value of your investment fluctuate day-to-day runs a high risk of failing to increase the value of your investment to the needed amount over time.

The bottom line is that the more time you have to invest, the more risk you should take. That doesn't mean you should grab your retirement nest egg and head to the nearest poker table, though. The risk should fall within your personal tolerance and with mutual funds it's easy to make sure that it does.

Terms, Terms, Terms

In the investment world, people classify their goals by the amount of time required to achieve them. There are three general time frames: short-term, medium-term, and long-term.

- **Short-term describes a time horizon of 0–5 years.**
- **Medium-term describes a time horizon of 6–10 years.**
- **Long-term describes a time horizon of 11 years or more.**

On the goal worksheet, you specify when you want each of your goals. Next you'll group your goals by time frame instead of by the exact number of years. This helps you prepare common investment strategies.

How Much Risk Is Right for You?

The appropriate level of risk for you depends on the time frames of your investment goals, your tolerance for risk, your age, and how much money you have outside your investment goals.

More Risk Brings More Return Over Time

With investment goals, time is the key. Remember the shoes versus the retirement. The only real difference between the two goals was their time frame: six months for the shoes, twenty years for the retirement. But aside from the goals themselves, you need to consider how you feel about risk, how old you are, and how much of your money is at stake.

How Much Time Do You Have?

Take a moment to look at your investment goals. If they are a long way off, accept a higher degree of risk with the knowledge that in the long run it will pay off. For your more immediate investment goals, temper that risk so that when the time comes to use the money, it will be worth what you want it to be.

Remember that the more time you have, the more day-to-day risk you can withstand. Little losses are compensated by steady gains over time. In fact, if you insist on too much stability, your money will probably not grow by enough to meet your long-term goals.

Categorize your goals by their terms. Goals that are 0 to 5 years away are short-term, those that are 6 to 10 years away are medium-term, and those that are 11 or more years away are long-term. Within each term, accept more risk as you increase the amount of time. For example, say you want to add an addition to your home in 6 years and put in a pool in 10 years. Both goals are classified as medium-term, but you should still accept more risk with the pool money than the home-improvement money. Why? Because the pool money has an additional 4 years to grow. It has a longer amount of time during which to recover from losses and profit from gains.

Now, these risk levels are not scientific. It appears that the home improvement should have 40 percent less risk than the pool, but figuring out risk is not that precise. It's important to know this when planning long-term goals because there is a limit to the amount of risk you should take. For instance, a goal that is thirty years away shouldn't necessarily be twice as risky as one that is fifteen years away, and maybe not riskier at all.

Luckily, because you're investing in mutual funds, you will never face anything terribly risky. Also, there are reliable tools to measure risk and you'll learn about four of them on page 19.

How Do You Feel About Investment Risks?

It's okay to expect a life free of financial terror. You might have read everything so far about how certain investments fluctuate in value from day to day but will rise over time, and be squirming in your seat. Perhaps a recurring vision of an account statement arriving in the mail from your mutual fund company with a number lower than the one that was there last month makes your eyes water and your mouth go dry. You're not alone.

You Don't Need a Test to Know How You Feel About Risk

Financial advisers would say that you have a "low risk tolerance." There are psychological investment tests that ask questions like "Would you place your last $10 bill on a blackjack table in Vegas or in a safe deposit box?" Personally, I'd put it toward postage for cover letters and résumés, but that's not the point. The point of those tests is to assess your risk tolerance.

I won't ask you a bunch of questions because I don't think they're necessary. It really comes down to one question: how much will it bother you to see the value of your account fluctuate from day to day? You know that those fluctuations will even out over the long term and that your investment will rise, but that might not be enough to comfort you in the short term. Only you know the answer.

Even though your gut feelings are important when considering risk, don't let them outweigh your better judgment. For example, if you are nervous about losing money but are a twenty-five-year-old saving for retirement, you need to give serious thought to investing in aggressive funds. Despite how you feel, the facts are that stocks perform better over long time periods than, say, a bank account. On the other hand, if you would place your last $10 bill on a blackjack table and are considering the same strategy for your retirement fund, you need to spend time examining the very real risk that you will lose all of your money. Though this is obviously an extreme example, there are funds that pose too much risk for certain goals. Even if you have a high tolerance for such risk, it might not be wise to expose yourself to it.

How Old Are You?

I know I spent all that time on page 7 explaining that goals matter, not age. However, it stands to reason that the older a person is, the less time he or she has to devote to long-term goals. Therefore, older people should tend toward investments that present less risk. This isn't to say that older people shouldn't tailor risk levels to their individual goals, just that they should keep their age in mind when defining their goals. Just how much of a time frame does a ninety-year-old have to work with? Nobody knows, but it's probably safest to invest for the short-term no matter what the goal is.

How Much Money Do You Have Outside of Your Investment Goals?

This is a good thing to keep in mind. If your investment money is a tiny slice of your overall budget, you can afford to up the risk a little because you don't have as much on the line. But if you are driving hard toward an important goal and are directing a huge portion of your income to it, be careful. It would be a shame to see that goal go up in smoke as your account balance goes down in flames. A quick way to decide how important this factor is in choosing a risk level for each of your goals is to ask how your life would be affected if the account were to disappear altogether. The chances of this happening with mutual funds is quite low, but the question forces you to think about how safe that money should be.

Choose an Acceptable Risk Level for Your Goals

Once you've got an idea for the amount of risk you're willing to accept for each of your investment goals, you can search among different mutual funds for one that suits your needs. I'll cover how to do that later. Your goal worksheet located at the back of this guidebook helps you assign a time frame and acceptable risk level to each of your goals. Here's what my sport coupe and college-funding goals would look like:

What You Want	Time Frame Short-term: 0–5 (years) Medium-term: 6–10 Long-term: Over 10	Acceptable Risk Level High, Medium, or Low
Lexus Sport Coupe	Short-term	Low
College Funding	Medium-term	Medium to High

Four Helpful Risk Measurements

To help you choose funds that fit your individual risk requirements, there are four good measurements to use. Each is a statistic used in Modern Portfolio Theory (MPT), which states that higher risk should bring higher rewards over time. The four measurements are sometimes grouped under the MPT heading.

The idea that risk is measurable and relates directly to reward (more risk, more reward over time), was first suggested in 1952 by a 25-year-old University of Chicago student named Harry Markowitz. Since then the idea has become an accepted truth.

Using the four measurements from MPT that are covered in this section, you can get a good feel for how a fund has behaved in the past. The measurements will give you a profile of fund styles and help you narrow the wide world of mutual funds to a manageable group.

Beta

A close cousin of risk is volatility, which is the measure of temporary fluctuations in the value of your investment. It generally happens that the riskier a mutual fund is, the greater its volatility or the amount that its NAV fluctuates.

For example, if you put your trusty $100 in a fund on Monday and by Wednesday it's only worth $75, you might begin to worry. By Friday your money might be up to $120 and back down to $90 the following Monday. You would be in an extremely volatile fund. Very few mutual funds fluctuate that much in price. You'd even be hard pressed to find an individual stock that fluctuated that much!

This kind of volatility seems risky because it's unpredictable. You never know what your money will be worth. The tendency over time might be for the price to increase, but on a day-to-day or month-to-month basis it's all over the board.

Mutual funds measure volatility with something called a beta coefficient, or just beta. A fund's beta is a calculation of how volatile the fund has been compared to an appropriate index, usually the Standard & Poor's 500 (S&P 500) index. An index is a collection of investments like stocks or bonds that represent a market. The S&P 500 index tracks the daily price changes of 80 percent of the stocks listed on the New York Stock Exchange and is considered a good measure of the market. A fund's beta helps you gauge whether the fund is more or less volatile than the S&P 500. You'll learn more about indexes on page 60.

A Lower Beta Is Better for the Short Term

Each index has a beta of 1. If a fund has a beta of 1.25, then it is 25 percent more volatile than its market index. That means that if the market is rising upward, the fund should outperform the market by 25 percent. When the market falls, the fund should fall 25 percent lower too. A stock fund that fluctuates 5 percent less than the S&P 500 has a beta of .95.

While "volatile" might sound bad at first, it isn't always. Would you rather invest your money in a fund that returns a constant 2 percent no matter what, or one that returns a range of numbers like 1 percent, 22 percent, 34 percent, and 15 percent? Naturally you'd rather have the second fund even though it is more volatile than the first, which faithfully returns 2 percent.

Also, long-term goals can be better served by volatile funds because losses are usually offset by gains. Moreover, funds that have extremely low volatility might not achieve the earnings you need for the long haul. No pain, no gain—if you can withstand volatility from year to year, you will probably be thankful for it in the long run.

As with risk in general, short-term goals are better served by funds with low volatility while long-term goals can withstand high volatility.

Alpha

Alpha takes the information contained in beta and compares it to a fund's performance. If it had been up to me to name each of these measurements, I would have flipped them around since alpha comes before beta in the Greek alphabet. You would think that beta should rely on information already established in alpha, but it doesn't. It's the other way around.

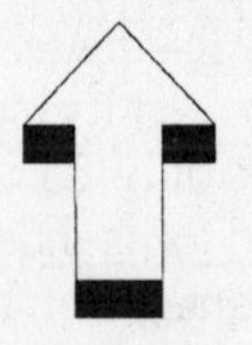

A Higher Alpha Is Better

An alpha of 0 means that the fund performed as expected for a fund of its volatility. So if it was a fund with a beta of 1.25, then it did indeed outperform its market by 25 percent in up markets and underperform it by 25 percent in down markets. An alpha greater than 0 means that the fund has performed better than expected given its beta. A growth stock fund with an alpha greater than 0 either maintained losses closer to those of the S&P 500 during a market decline than its beta would suggest, or it returned more than it should have when the market rose. If the fund's beta was 1.25, maybe it beat the S&P 500 by 35 percent in a rising market instead of the 25 percent you would expect. Or, the fund might have lost only 5 percent more than the S&P 500 when the market fell.

The ideal fund would have a low beta and a high alpha. However, a high beta and a very high alpha would be good too.

In sweeping terms, a higher alpha is better. However, some of the best-performing funds have negative alphas because short-term volatility can penalize a fund when alpha is measured, while over the long term the fund is a winner. Also, since beta is only a rough assessment of risk and the alpha score is based on how the fund performed relative to its beta, an imprecise beta can result in an imprecise alpha. That means a fund that did very well but had a high beta would end up with an average or low alpha.

Given these factors, alpha isn't a surefire method of choosing a fund but can be helpful. It's similar to a certain car winning the *Motor Trend* Car of the Year award. Sure, it's a good thing to have, but that doesn't necessarily mean the car is best for your situation. There are other factors to consider.

R-Squared

Though it sounds esoteric, R-squared (sometimes written R^2) is pretty straightforward. It tells you what amount of a fund's return is based on the return of its index. Remember from the explanation of beta that an index is a collection of stocks or bonds that represent a market. While beta is usually measured against the S&P 500 stock index, R-squared is measured against an index that most closely tracks the kinds of investments that a given fund owns. An R-squared of 100 says that the fund merely duplicated its index while an R-squared of 25 says that only 25 percent of the fund's return is attributed to its index.

It Ain't That Bad

If you like a certain stock fund that has an R-squared of 100, you'd be better off in an index fund. An index fund uses a computer to automatically invest in the stocks or bonds tracked by its index. The reason you should choose an index fund over a fund with an R-squared of 100 managed by a person is that the fund manager has only invested in the fund's index anyway. Since the index fund is managed by a computer, its expenses are lower than the fund managed by a person. So you would save money by investing in the inexpensive index fund. The index fund return will also have an R-squared of 100—just like the fund managed by a person—since it is wholly defined by its index. You will read more about index funds on page 59.

If a fund has an R-squared of 0, then its performance is independent of the benchmark index. That means that if the index rises over a period of time, the fund won't necessarily follow. Likewise, when the index falls, the fund might be soaring in the clouds.

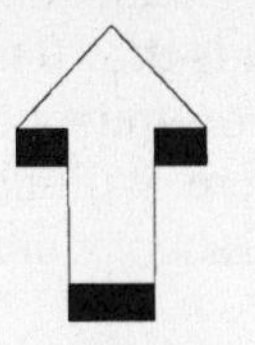

A Higher R-Squared Indicates That a Fund Is Closely Tied to Its Index

R-squared is best used to see what index a fund most closely follows. By knowing that information, you can choose whether you want to assemble a portfolio of funds that represents a diverse section of the investment market. For example, if you already own a fund that has an R-squared of 95.3 against the S&P 500, you wouldn't want to invest in another fund with a high R-squared against the S&P 500. Why? Because you are already following that index with the fund you own. If you want to place more money in the S&P 500, just buy additional shares in the fund you already own.

If, on the other hand, you want to diversify your money by investing some of it in a different part of the market, you should look for a fund that has a high R-squared against a different index. Perhaps a fund that has an R-squared over 90 against the Russell 2000, which is an index that tracks small companies, would be better for you.

Now, R-squared isn't as bad as it seemed, is it?

Standard Deviation

While beta measures a fund's volatility relative to the S&P 500, standard deviation measures a fund's pure volatility. The two are related but different in an important way. With beta, a fund is considered volatile if it is more volatile than the S&P 500. With standard deviation, a fund is considered volatile or stable based solely on the consistency of its own monthly returns.

The standard deviation is the percentage range that a fund's monthly return has "deviated" from its average return, or mean. To compensate for variations, standard deviation is considered accurate 67 percent of the time. For example, if a fund's average annual return is 10 percent and it has a standard deviation of 5, you know that 67 percent of the time its return should range from 5 percent to 15 percent, which is the 10 percent average annual return plus or minus the 5 percent standard deviation. There will have been months that it fell outside the range at either end of the spectrum.

A Lower Standard Deviation Indicates a More Consistent Fund

Doubling a fund's standard deviation increases the reliability of the measurement from 67 percent of the time to 95 percent of the time. So using the example above, double the standard deviation of 5 to get 10. To find the lower range limit, subtract the 10 from the fund's 10 percent annual return to get 0. To find the upper range limit, add the 10 to the fund's 10 percent annual return to get 20. Your calculations reveal that 95 percent of the time the fund's returns should range from 0 percent to 20 percent.

For two funds identical in all regards but standard deviation, you'd prefer the one with a low standard deviation because it has been more consistent.

Asset Allocation

Dividing All Your Money Among Asset Classes

You already know that by investing in mutual funds, you diversify your money across many different holdings. That's one of the chief benefits of mutual funds.

On a bigger scale is asset allocation, which is dividing all your money among different funds that combine to make your investment mix appropriate for its time frame.

Two Decisions to Make

There are two decisions to make when allocating your money. The first is deciding how much money to place in each of the three major asset classes you learned about in the beginning of this chapter: stocks, bonds, and the money market. As a mutual fund investor, you won't actually be buying the stocks, bonds, and money market instruments but will be selecting from funds that focus on one of the three asset classes. The second decision is choosing how much of your money to place in international investments.

The Three Asset Classes

Each asset class has benefits and is appropriate for certain objectives and age groups. Allocation is the division of your money across the asset classes and should be changed at different times during your life. It might also be different for each of your investment goals.

Each asset class performs better in certain economic environments and over different time periods, though none is best all the time. The average annual return of each class from 1926 to 1993 in the U.S. was: stocks 10.3 percent, bonds 5 percent, and money market 3.7 percent as shown in this graph:

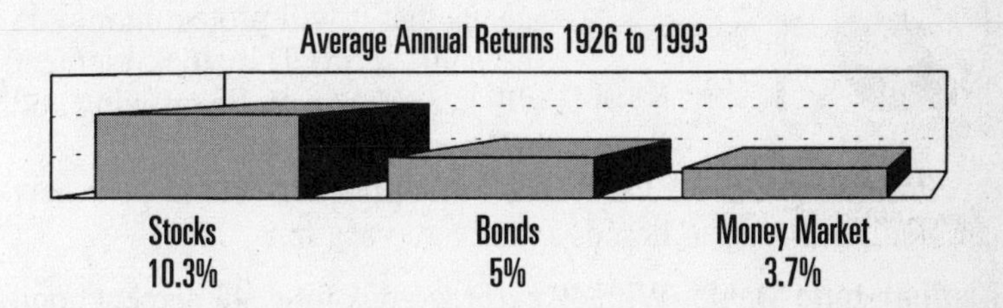

Looking at the graph, stocks seem the best choice, but it's the long time period that makes them look so good. Recall that stocks are the riskiest of the three classes and that time rewards risk. That means that stock funds make better long-term investments than funds targeting the other two asset classes.

For your short- and medium-term goals, the concentration of bond and money market funds should increase. For your very short-term goals, you shouldn't own any stock funds but instead put your money in safe places like bank accounts or a pure money market fund, both of which pose very little risk and similar returns.

For example, it's a good idea to have six months of pay set aside in an emergency account that lets you easily get to the money. Since you never know when you'll need the emergency money, it would not be wise to put it in a risky stock fund whose shares might be worth less than you paid for them when you get your money. Choose a bank savings account or a money market fund instead. Doing so guarantees that the money will be there when you need it and won't be worth less than what you invested. You don't want to be drawing from one of your stock mutual funds to pay for groceries.

Look at the portfolios below. They illustrate a good mixture of the asset classes for different time frames, goals, and stages in life. Keep your own goals in mind and see if any of these match the way you would like your money invested. There are many other possibilities, but all are variations of these basic portfolios.

Short-term Safe This portfolio is comprised of 25 percent stock fund, 40 percent bond fund, and 35 percent money market fund. It is low-risk and focuses on bonds and the money market, which means that it will protect money in the short term. The stock element will keep the portfolio growing and help outpace inflation.

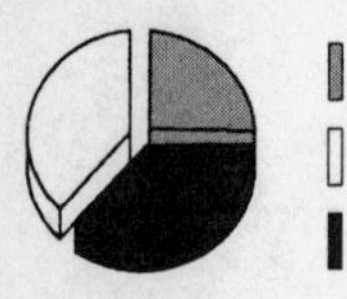

Possible goals well served by this portfolio would be a new car, additions to your home, or a dream vacation.

Medium-term Stable With 40 percent stock fund, 40 percent bond fund, and 20 percent money market fund, this portfolio will perform well for medium-term goals. The stocks and bonds will help the investment stay ahead of inflation, and the money market will keep volatility within a comfortable range. An investor attracted to this mixture would be able to tolerate fluctuations in the portfolio's value in exchange for greater returns over time.

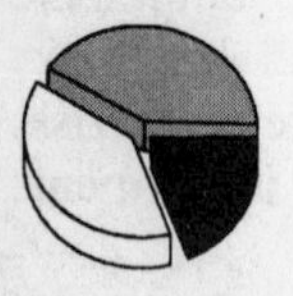

Some goals to consider for this portfolio would be college tuition for your twelve-year-old son, a down payment on a new home, or preparation for a business you hope to start in the future.

Long-term Ambitious No problems for the long haul: 65 percent stock fund, 30 percent bond fund, and 5 percent money market fund. This mixture will outpace inflation and grow with time. Investors here should ignore short-term losses because they will be unaffected when it comes time to redeem their shares. Just in case, however, a tiny piece of the money market will soften volatility.

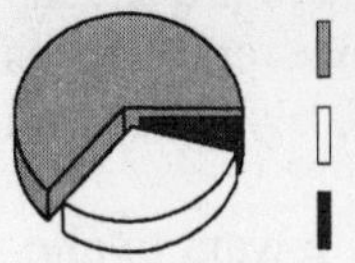

Appropriate goals for this portfolio are retirement, college tuition for your two-year-old daughter, or your second marriage. Just kidding about the marriage.

Long-term Aggressive Go for the gusto! 100 percent stock funds across the board. Inflation isn't a concern, and the growth potential is at its highest. The downside is that short-term losses are inevitable and could be severe. These investors expect a turbulent journey but are confident that they will be rewarded in the end. They examine the value of their investment on an annual basis, but probably not monthly or daily.

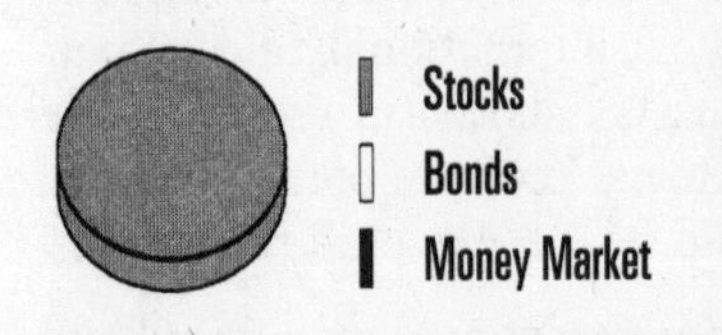

The main goal with this portfolio is retirement.

Going Global

The sample portfolios above divide your money among the three basic asset classes. That's the first decision you need to make when allocating your money. The second is deciding how much of your money to allocate to international stock funds.

International stock funds are appropriate for long-term goals. Foreign markets do not correlate 100 percent with the U.S. market, which means that when our economy is in a slump, foreign economies might be booming. The balance you achieve between the two markets is further diversification of your portfolio, which reduces your overall risk. Just as money market funds help your portfolio when stock funds take a dive, international funds can help your portfolio when the U.S. market takes a dive.

Many of the best investment opportunities are located overseas. By allocating part of your portfolio to international funds, you can take advantage of those opportunities. There are special risks associated with international investing, however, such as currency fluctuation and political instability. You will learn all about international mutual funds on page 48.

For now, give thought to how much money you want to allocate to international funds for each of your long-term goals. Consider how diversified you want your portfolios to be. Remember that the longer you have to invest, the more risk you can afford to take because time smoothes out short-term ups and downs. A goal that is at least 10 years away can tolerate swings in the international market and profit from the overall boost that foreign investments can provide.

The ideal mix of international funds to domestic funds is between 70 percent U.S. to 30 percent international, and 50 percent U.S. to 50 percent international as shown in these sample portfolios. The international investments keep the portfolios solid when the U.S. is faltering and should increase overall returns.

Light International With 30 percent international stock fund and 70 percent domestic stock fund, this mixture is good for goals that are between 10 and 15 years away. By keeping the bulk of the portfolio at home, these investors keep closer tabs on their market. The 30 percent international component is enough to lessen U.S. market fluctuations.

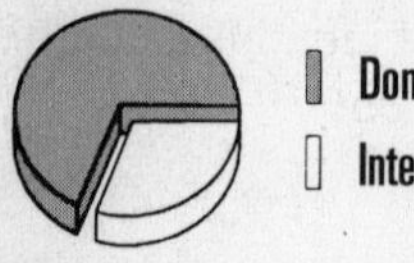

Heavy International This is best for goals that are more than 15 years away. A 50 percent domestic to 50 percent international mixture means this portfolio sees the world as one big market. This portfolio seeks opportunity wherever it occurs and should profit from that strategy in the end.

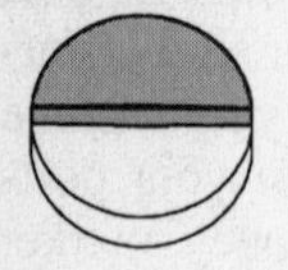

What Allocation Is Right for You?

After looking at the sample portfolios in the previous section, you should understand how the various asset classes complement one another and that long-term goals should have part of their portfolios invested internationally. The varying degrees of risk and reward are important to keep in mind as you decide on a mixture for your goals. Here's a table that summarizes the three asset classes and international stocks:

Asset Class	Best Time Frame	Relative Risk	Potential Return
Stocks	Long-term	High	High
Bonds	Medium-term	Medium	Medium
Money Market	Short-term	Low	Low
International Stocks	Long-term	High	High

Revisit your goal worksheet, this time noting a mixture of the three asset classes and international stocks that you think will be right for you. Be sure to read the next chapter, which explains each type of fund in more detail. It's especially important that you understand the section on international and global investing, which begins on page 48. Here's how I'd allocate my sport coupe, college funding, and retirement goals:

What You Want	Mutual Fund Allocation Percentages			
	Stocks	Bonds	Money Market	International
Lexus Sport Coupe	25	40	35	0
College Funding	50	20	0	30
Retirement	50	0	0	50

Rebalancing Your Allocation

As your investments expand and contract with the market, you might find that your original allocation gets shifted. To compensate, you should rebalance your mixture.

For example, let's say you have 50 percent of your money in stock funds and 50 percent in money market funds. If the stock funds you own surge forward, then your overall investment will increase. But the proportion of your money invested in stocks would rise so that your new mixture might be 60 percent stock and only 40 percent money market. There are three things you can do to regain your original mix:

1. Add to the money market side of your portfolio.
2. Move money from your stock funds into the money market.
3. Sell stock fund shares until the proportion of those remaining equals your target.

No matter which option you choose, you'll enjoy the advantage of either buying one class low or selling another high. How? Look at the example above. If you choose option 1, you invest new money into the money market side of your portfolio, which has not increased by as much as the stock side—you're buying low. If you choose option 2, you sell part of the stock side of your portfolio, which has increased, to buy a larger stake in the money market side, which has not increased by as much—you're selling high and buying low. If you choose option 3, you sell part of the stock side of your portfolio, which has increased—you're selling high.

Time to Rebalance

Rebalancing is a good practice because it insures that you maintain the risk and reward harmony you decided was appropriate for your goals. If the stocks in your portfolio shrink to a smaller percentage, you might have trouble achieving the earnings for your goal. If the stocks exceed their percentage, you will face more risk. An annual rebalancing helps prevent both.

Changing Your Allocation

For especially long-term goals like retirement and college tuition, it's appropriate to change your allocation as you near the goal. While retirement might be thirty years away now, it won't always be.

Take the long-term aggressive portfolio. With 100 percent stock it's obviously hoping to smooth out short-term gains and losses with an upward trend over time. But as you approach sixty and anticipate retiring, you don't want to risk needing your money when it's in a market valley.

It makes sense to assess your allocation from time to time. If you are unhappy with the returns you've been getting or nervous that the bottom is about to fall out of what has been a good thing, adjust your money. There's nothing wrong with converting the long-term aggressive portfolio into the medium-term stable. Likewise if the ambitious fund isn't holding up to the talk of your friends at dinner parties, you could always move up to the aggressive mixture.

Start Now

It's always the right time to invest in mutual funds. Whether you feel guilty for waiting so long or doubt that you need to worry about investments at your young age, start now. You'll thank yourself for it.

Power of Compounding

The growth of money is a deceptive thing because you're most excited about your investment when you first make it. But that's generally when it does the least. Now and then somebody catches a shooting star and you hear tales of stock purchased for pennies and sold a week later for dollars, but they're the exception. Most of us put our money away and watch it grow slowly.

Money Compounding

Compounding is powerful, though. Returns build on previous returns, so late years produce much more than early years. If you put $100 in a mutual fund that returns 10 percent a year and you reinvest all distributions, after ten years you'll have $259. After twenty years you'll have $673, and after forty years you'll have $4,526. The return from year one was $10 while the return from year forty was $411. The increase gets progressively bigger because returns build on earnings from previous years in addition to your principle.

For example, that $100 turned into $4,526 in forty years thanks to compounding. If you took the 10 percent annual return and placed it in a separate account that didn't pay any interest, you would end up with much less money. Ten percent of $100 is $10. After forty years of collecting the $10 annual return, you would have amassed only $400. Adding your initial $100 investment would give you a grand total of $500. Not much compared to the $4,526 you would have earned by taking advantage of compounded returns. Why the huge difference? Because compounding earns returns on your previous returns.

Once again, time is your best friend. No matter where you are in life, start your investment program now to take advantage of the time available. If you have children and can afford the extra payments, consider starting a fund for them when they're infants that will swell considerably by the time they leave home. You can always keep their money if they disappoint you.

Power of Regular Investing

In addition to beginning your investment program now, you should also contribute to it regularly. By doing so you'll develop a habit of saving, and it also makes good business sense.

Dollar-Cost Averaging

When you invest the same amount of money on a regular basis, the average cost of your shares usually decreases. This is called dollar-cost averaging. It forces your money to buy more shares when the price is lower and fewer shares when the price is higher. Look at this six-month investment program:

Date	Investment	NAV Per Share	Shares Purchased
January 15	$100	$25	4
February 15	$100	$20	5
March 15	$100	$10	10
April 15	$100	$15	6.7
May 15	$100	$25	4
June 15	$100	$30	3.3
Totals	$600	$20.83 (average)	33

Average market NAV per share	$20.83
Average NAV paid per share	$18.18
Average savings per share	$2.65

This investor sent $100 on the fifteenth of each month regardless of the fund's NAV. At the end of six months, he calculated the average NAV he paid per share by dividing his $600 investment by the 33 shares he owns. In the end he saved an average of $2.65 on each share he purchased just by sending the same amount of money on a regular basis.

Dollar-cost averaging doesn't guarantee anything. It's possible to continue saving money per share as the price drops straight into the dirt. Sure, you would have bought more shares when the price was down, but the fact still remains that the shares are worthless.

Nonetheless, dollar-cost averaging is the simplest way for investors to build wealth over time. No investment strategy can guarantee good results, but dollar-cost averaging is certainly preferable to guessing the best time to invest. In most cases dollar-cost averaging will lower the average price per share, and it is less risky than moving large amounts of money all at once.

Together They Really Pay Off

This is where it gets good.

When you combine the benefits of compounding with the strategy of regular investing, you are well on your way to a prosperous future. As you set aside money each month, you will purchase shares at a good average price. Your principal will continue growing, which will add to the effect of the compounding. Any distributions that you receive can go back into your investment so that you're making money three ways.

Jay Gould made a fortune in our nation's budding railroad industry and was often approached for investment advice. Gould's minister asked where he should invest his $30,000 life savings. In strict confidence, Gould recommended Missouri Pacific stock. The minister invested his entire life savings, watched the stock spike upward briefly, then saw it bottom out months later. He angrily delivered the news to Gould, who immediately wrote the minister a check for $40,000. Only then did the minister sheepishly confess having told many members of the congregation about Gould's investment tip. "Oh, I know that," Gould replied. "They were the ones I was after."

3 A Fund for Every Occasion

Since mutual funds gather investors with common goals, you might have guessed that there are several different kinds of funds. There have to be because people have different personalities and goals. The variety of funds reflects this diversity among people. You learned in the last chapter about the three basic investment objectives: growth, income, and stability. Within each objective there are different kinds of funds. Many mutual funds combine the objectives, the most popular combination being growth and income.

This chapter outlines different kinds of funds available under each objective and also covers funds that combine objectives. Here is a table of the funds explained in this chapter:

Fund Category	Invests Primarily In	Best For
Growth	Large Company Stocks	Long-term or Medium-term
Aggressive Growth	Small Company Stocks	Long-term
Sector	Stocks from a Market Sector	Long-term
Income	Bonds and High-Dividend Stocks	Medium-term or Short-term
Growth and Income	Stocks and Bonds	Long-term or Medium-term
Money Market	Money Market Instruments	Short-term
International and Global	International and U.S. Securities	Long-term
Asset Allocation	All Asset Classes	Long-term or Medium-term

Fund Category	Invests Primarily In	Best For
Balanced	All Asset Classes	Long-term or Medium-term
Index	Stocks or Bonds from an Index	Long-term or Medium-term
Life Cycle	All Asset Classes	Long-term
Precious Metals	Precious Metal and Related Stocks	Long-term
Social Conscience	"Responsible" Company Stocks	Long-term

Feeling Blown Away? Don't Sweat It. It's Easy to Find a Fund That's Right for You.

Growth

A growth fund tries to increase the value of its portfolio by purchasing stocks whose prices will rise. It isn't concerned with collecting interest or dividend payments. When you place money in a growth fund, you hope to come back at a later date and find that your money has "grown" to a larger amount. With this objective in mind, growth funds concentrate on owning stocks. Stocks are sometimes referred to as equities, so you might see growth funds called either stock funds or equity funds.

What Is a Stock?

Stock represents ownership in a company. When you exchange money for a share of stock, you have contributed to the company's capital, and in return you receive shares of ownership. Generally, if a company is successful and its earnings grow, its stock value will rise. If it encounters hard times, its stock value will fall.

What Is a Dividend?

Stockholders are often entitled to a share of the company's profit in the form of dividends. Dividends are declared at a certain dollar amount per share so that the more shares you own the more you earn. For example, if IBM declares $.25 stock dividend and you own 100 shares of IBM stock, you will receive $25.

When a mutual fund buys stock in a company, it buys a lot. By doing so it can reduce the cost associated with purchasing stock, such as brokerage commissions. Growth funds are not always looking for stocks that declare dividends (see text boxes on the previous page) because a dividend is considered current income, not growth. Instead, they are seeking stock in companies that are doing well in their industry and will probably grow. This increases the likelihood of the company's stock price rising. When that happens, the value of the mutual fund shares rises too.

Growth Funds

Growth funds are the basic stock-buying funds. They are what the first mutual funds were and the most popular fund in America, Fidelity Magellan, which manages more than $50 billion, is a growth fund.

Growth funds invest primarily in companies that everybody knows like General Electric, IBM, Intel, Microsoft, and Coca Cola, plus a few that you might not know. Stocks in companies that are household names and trusted investments are called blue chip stocks and are considered safer than the smaller companies that an aggressive growth fund would buy. Like most investment generalizations, this one doesn't always hold true. Witness the decline of IBM stock from its glory days selling well over $100 per share to its 1993 low of around $40 and climb back up to the $100 mark in 1995. Even faithful performers take roller-coaster rides now and then.

Growth funds are usually very diversified. When you see a statement of holdings for a growth mutual fund, the stock in which the fund has invested most of its money will probably represent only about 2 percent of the fund's total assets. It's not uncommon for a growth fund to own stock in more than 100 companies! Of all stock funds put together, four of the most common stocks to own are General Electric, AT&T, Motorola, and Intel. Yet even these big names each only occupy about one half of 1 percent of total stock fund investments.

A growth fund should be thought of as a long-term

investment. The trend of the stock market is to rise over time, and growth funds should ride that trend. They will probably not produce eye-popping returns in a given year, but over time they will prove reliable.

Aggressive Growth Funds

Aggressive growth funds try to grow more than growth funds by buying stock in small companies. These represent a greater risk because they lack the resources of a huge corporation, but they have potential for greater growth because they're often young and just beginning their product cycle with higher rates of sales and earnings increases ahead. An aggressive growth fund hopes to buy the stock of these companies before they realize full maturity.

Small companies can be quite risky. A lot of them are banking on the success of a single product or a handful of products. If one gloomy news report stifles sales or a single shipment of parts arrives late, the entire company is at risk. Of course, investors are hoping that the single product on which the company is betting its existence sells like sunscreen at a nude beach. But you never know for sure.

Small Companies Can Leave You on a Limb in the Short Term

Some aggressive growth funds engage in riskier practices, like buying unregistered stock, writing options, and using borrowed money to buy more than they can actually afford at the moment. These kinds of risks are generally rewarded in the long run but are not a good idea for short-term investors.

All this "aggression" leads to a huge variation in returns. A fund might double in value one year only to lose 40 percent the next. Aggressive growth funds typically rise more than other funds in bull markets and fall more than others in bear markets.

Bull Market: When Stocks Are Rising

Bear Market: When Stocks Are Falling

Lobster Market: A Place to Buy Lobster

Remember the beta measurement you learned about on page 20? Aggressive growth funds usually have a beta greater than 1.

Sector Funds

Sector funds are some of the most aggressive mutual funds available. They purchase the stock of companies that operate in a narrowly defined sector or industry of the economy.

To invest in a sector fund, you would have to feel strongly that its part of the economy is going to perform especially well in upcoming months or years. This is as close to buying individual stocks as mutual funds get. Not only do sector funds involve the judgment of the mutual fund manager, they also rely on the investor's outlook for a particular industry.

A technology sector fund might buy stock in companies like Compaq, Lotus, and Oracle. A utilities fund might look toward phone companies and electricity producers. A biotechnology fund could acquire shares of Genentech and Biogen. As you can see, sector funds are very focused and require accurate predictions on the potential of a specific industry.

Similar to the trend with individual stocks, sector fund investors tend to get in at market peaks and get out in the bottom of market valleys. Psychology and emotion get in the way because everybody brags about industries when they're booming and grumbles about them when they're lagging.

Ironically, the grumbling times are best for buying, and the bragging times are best for selling. But our minds don't tell us that. If your best friend approached you and said, "I just lost $500 in my biotech fund," would you want to run out and buy shares? Probably not.

Sector funds are best for experienced investors who can afford to lose money when they misjudge the market.

There is a type of international mutual fund called a regional fund that targets parts of the world, just like a sector fund targets parts of the U.S. economy. You'll read about regional funds on page 56.

Income

An income fund tries to provide current income rather than growth. That means that if you send an income fund $100, it would rather earn a monthly amount on that money than try turning it into $200.

Income funds invest in bonds from government agencies or corporations since bonds provide income in the form of interest payments. Some funds also buy stocks that produce income through dividend payments. Because of these stock investments, some income funds can produce growth as well. You'll learn more about income funds that also purchase stock in the growth and income section on page 46.

What Is a Bond?

A bond is an obligation by a government or a company to pay back borrowed money and interest by a certain date. When you buy a bond, you are lending money to the bond issuer.

In bond language the loan principal is called face value or par value, the interest percentage is called coupon rate, and the actual rate of return is called yield. So if you paid $1,000 for a $1,000 face-value bond with a coupon rate of 10 percent, it would pay $100 a year in interest, and its yield would be the coupon rate (100 ÷ 1,000 = 10 percent).

If you paid only $800 for the same bond you would still receive $100 a year in interest from the bond issuer, but your yield would be 13 percent (100 ÷ 800 = 13 percent). The fact that bond issuers always pay the coupon rate against the face value is the reason bonds are "fixed-income" investments.

The amount of time until the bond issuer pays back the face value is called the bond's maturity and can range from 3 months to 30 years or even longer. Bond holders receive interest payments until maturity, when they are paid the entire face value at once.

Bonds are categorized by their credit quality, which is an assessment of the financial strength and reliability of the bond issuer. The better the credit quality, the lower the interest on the bond. Conversely, less reliable

issuers need to offer higher interest to attract buyers.

Since bonds pay a fixed return, they become less valuable as interest rates rise. When interest rates fall, bonds become more valuable because their return will not decline. Think of interest rates being on one side of a see-saw and bond prices on the other. When one goes up, the other goes down.

This see-saw relationship isn't difficult to understand. Just take interest rates to the extreme and see how you would behave. If your local bank pays 25 percent interest, will you buy a bond with a 13 percent yield? Of course not. Therefore the bond is not valuable. If your bank suddenly drops its interest rate to 5 percent, the bond with a 13-percent yield looks pretty good. Thus, it becomes more valuable.

Don't sweat the details of owning individual bonds. You're going to buy through a mutual fund. It's good to know the basics, which I've covered in this text box, but let the fund manager figure out the details!

There are two important differences between owning bonds yourself and owning shares in a bond mutual fund. First, although bonds mature, bond funds don't. You can hold shares in a bond fund forever and they will never mature because the fund is constantly selling old bonds and buying new ones with a different maturity. Second, bonds pay fixed amounts of interest on specified dates during the year. Bond funds pay a monthly interest that fluctuates. A lot of funds average these payments for a smoother income stream.

Government Bond Funds

Money is lent to the U.S. government by purchasing "Treasuries." The three types of treasuries are Treasury bills, Treasury bonds, and Treasury notes. All are basically risk-free because the government will honor its debt. Treasuries are backed by the "full faith and credit" of the U.S. government, but with a surging national debt some people wonder how reliable that faith and credit is. For now, though, Treasuries are considered risk-free.

Government bond funds purchase Treasuries. Although the government will always pay what it agreed to pay, the price of bonds might drop if interest rates rise. That means that fund shareholders could see a lower NAV.

Government bond funds usually specialize in certain maturities. With bonds, short-term is considered 0–5 years, intermediate term is 6–15 years, and long-term is over 15 years. The longer the maturity specialization, the riskier the fund because there's more time for interest rates to fluctuate.

I use the word risky here only relative to other bond funds. A government bond fund is not risky at all compared to a growth fund, for example. In fact, many investors use government bond funds when interest rates are falling or already down. Banks and the money market don't pay much in such times, but government bonds offer a safe way to pick up a decent return.

Mortgage-Backed Funds

Another kind of government bond encourages investment in America's housing market. Three federal agencies purchase mortgages from banks, throw them all in a pool, and then sell shares of the mortgage pool to investors. It works like a mutual fund of home mortgages.

Each government agency has a nickname. There's "Ginnie Mae" for the Government National Mortgage Association (GNMA), "Fannie Mae" for the Federal National Mortgage Association (FNMA), and "Freddie Mac" for the Federal Home Loan Mortgage Association (don't ask me how they got Freddie Mac from that).

Mutual funds that buy mortgage-backed securities generally pay better than those that buy Treasuries, and the risk is still negligible because the government agencies guarantee their bonds. The main risk with mortgage-backed funds is that when interest rates drop, homeowners will refinance. This replaces high-paying mortgages with low-paying ones, and the fund's yield will decrease.

Municipal Bond Funds

These funds produce tax-free income. That's right, tax-free. People in high tax brackets love the municipal (or just "muni") bond fund market, even if it sometimes achieves lower returns, because the tax advantages are so appealing.

Munis buy bonds issued by smaller government units like states and cities to fund schools, roads, and hospitals. To encourage this type of investment, the government has made income from it exempt from taxes.

Okay, like everything else related to taxes, there are exceptions to the tax-free status of muni bond funds. The income is always exempt from federal taxes but might be taxed by your state. If your state has a low income tax, the drain on your investment might be negligible. But for the high tax states like California and New York, the state tax can be a serious problem.

To overcome this problem, some fund companies offer single-state muni bond funds. By keeping all of their investments within one state, these funds guarantee that any income they produce is exempt from the taxes of that state, in addition to federal taxes. For example, a person living in Los Angeles could purchase a California tax-free income fund and be assured that they won't pay any taxes on their earnings. Of course, the drawback to owning investments from a single state is that if the state hits hard economic times, your returns could suffer. A muni fund that isn't restricted to a single state can soften the blow of a faltering state economy by investing in states that are doing well.

Municipal bond funds don't usually pay as well as other bond funds, but the tax advantages can outweigh the lower return. This, of course, depends on your tax bracket and the amount of money you invest. The higher your tax bracket, the more advantageous it is to receive tax-free income.

How Good Is Tax-free?

That depends on your tax bracket. Here's a standard formula to determine whether a lower tax-free return is better than a higher taxable one:

- **Subtract your tax bracket from 100.**

- **Divide the tax-free interest rate by the number you got in the previous step. The answer is the taxable rate that would give you the same yield as the tax-free rate.**

For example, say your tax bracket is 28 percent and you are trying to decide between a 10 percent taxable account and a 7 percent tax-free account. 100 minus 28 gives you 72. Divide 7 by 72 and you get .097 or 9.7 percent. That means that the tax-free account gives you a smaller return because 9.7 is less than 10. So tax-free isn't always the best option.

Corporate Bond Funds

These funds purchase bonds issued by corporations looking to raise money. The risk associated with this type of fund depends on the quality of the bonds it purchases. Also, corporations can "call" their bonds. That means that if interest rates fall and new bonds can be issued at a lower interest, the corporation might "call" back the higher-paying bonds to save money. When this happens, the mutual fund receives a little more than the face value of the bond, but must reinvest the money at lower interest rates than it previously earned.

The health of the corporation issuing bonds can change after the bonds have been purchased, thereby affecting the worth of the bonds. For example, if a corporation is going to purchase another corporation and take on lots of debt in the process, it won't be as financially healthy as it had been before. Nobody wants to lend money to somebody who has too much debt, and when your mutual fund buys a corporation's bonds, it is lending the corporation money. If the corporation overextends itself, its perceived quality level will decrease and so will the value of its bonds. Your shares in the corporate bond fund might decrease too.

Sometimes corporate bond funds buy U.S. Treasuries to maintain the quality promised to their investors. There are times when the yield from corporate bonds and Treasuries are very close, and the increased safety of Treasuries makes them more attractive than the bonds.

Zero-Coupon Bond Funds

"Zeros" are bonds from the government or a corporation that earn interest but don't pay it until maturity. However, holders of these bonds pay taxes on the unpaid interest each year. Zeros are the evil twin of municipal bonds. Munis pay the money without the taxes; zeros tax the money without the payments.

So why would any fund choose to buy zeros? Because they are usually sold at a deep discount, since they won't be making any interest payments until maturity. If the discount is substantial, the zero can overcome the tax disadvantage and have an overall yield higher than interest-paying bonds.

One way to get around the tax situation with zero funds is to own them in a tax-deferred account, like an Individual Retirement Account (IRA). The problem is that tax-deferred accounts usually have long-term goals in mind, such as retirement, and over the long term it is better to own the zeros themselves instead of a zero fund. The reason is that if you bought a zero-coupon bond itself from a broker and had it placed in a tax-deferred account, you wouldn't pay a cent until that bond matures and you withdraw the money. The zero doesn't make any payments, and the tax-deferred account shields you from paying taxes. But with a zero-coupon bond fund, you would pay annual fund expenses even though you don't pay taxes. You'll learn more about tax-deferred accounts in the retirement section on page 115.

Where does that leave zero-coupon bond funds? They are usually the most responsive to the see-saw relationship that bonds have to interest rates. That means that they make sense for short- to medium-term goals when interest rates are declining.

Junk Bond Funds

Junk bonds are the riskiest of all bonds because they are issued from unstable companies with weak credit ratings. Of course, that means they have the highest potential return.

In declining markets, junk bonds tend to default and these funds lose money. In rising markets, these funds can do very well. All mutual funds buy a lot of different investments, but it's particularly important for junk bond funds to do so because their investments run a high risk of default. A fund that owns a lot of junk bonds can escape being affected by an occasional default because its earnings will be buoyed by the successful bonds in its portfolio.

Growth and Income

A growth and income fund tries to get the best of both worlds. Some people assume that it's the smartest way to go because, after all, investors in growth and income funds are making money both ways. They should expect twice the returns, right? Not exactly. The returns from growth and income funds are more like what you'd expect from a conservative growth fund. However, growth and income funds tend to be more stable because they buy a mixture of low-risk money market instruments and bonds in addition to stocks.

Growth and income fund managers look for investments that provide both current income and long-term growth. These could be stocks in companies that are doing well and pay a dividend. For example, a fund that owned stock in General Electric and received dividend checks from the company while the price of its stock rose would be achieving both growth and income with GE.

Most growth and income funds decide on a combination of dividend-paying stocks and bonds. Depending on the specific fund's objective and degree of risk, the ratio of stocks to bonds will vary. For example, a riskier fund that wants to emphasize long-term growth would place more of its money in stocks than in bonds. A fund that primarily wants to create a steady stream of income but would also like its investor's principal to grow would place more of its money in bonds than in stocks.

Money Market

Funds seeking absolute stability invest in the money market. Professional managers for growth or income funds often move

Money Market Funds Are Safe Places

part of their fund's money into "cash" for safety. When they say cash, they mean the money market.

Like an income fund, a money market fund tries to create a high current income while preserving your initial investment. The difference is that a money market fund is safer than an income fund and therefore doesn't usually pay as much.

Money market funds are the most popular type of mutual fund because they're similar to a checking account with interest. They're a safe place to put money when you're saving for a short-term goal like spring vacation and don't have time to weather stock market fluctuations.

What Is the Money Market?

The money market consists of securities that are a lot like bonds. The main difference is that money market securities have much shorter maturities than bonds do. Some mature in one day! Money market instruments are often referred to as cash instruments, or just cash. Typical money market instruments include Treasury bills, certificates of deposit, commercial paper (short-term financing for companies), repurchase agreements, and banker's acceptances. All are just different kinds of loans.

As with stocks and bonds, you don't need to know the details of the money market because the mutual fund manager will handle everything.

Unlike a bank account, money market funds are not federally insured. That shouldn't scare you, though. Nobody has ever lost money in one. Some banks offer insured bank money market accounts, but they pay about 1 percent less than a money market mutual fund and there is little reason for the extra caution. Money market mutual funds are very safe investments. They're convenient too. Most will offer you checks or debit cards that you can use just as you would for your regular checking account. The money you place in a money market mutual fund is safe, always available, and earns an attractive return based on short-term interest rates.

The reason money market mutual funds pay more than bank money market accounts is that banks offer a managed rate. Your bank pays only the interest necessary to be competitive with other banks and keep you happy. If its interest is too low, you'll take your money elsewhere, but all banks want to offer you as low an interest rate as possible to save themselves money. Therefore, they tend to settle around an interest rate that is somewhat lower than the market rate. A money market mutual fund, on the other hand, pays you everything that it's able to earn from the money market. It wants to pay you as much as possible because the value of your account will grow, you'll want to invest more, and the fund can earn more on its management fee, which is a percentage of the money you have invested. You'll read about fees and other fund expenses on page 73.

Remember how the NAV of shares you purchase in growth or income funds fluctuates from day to day? In a money market fund that's not the case. Each share is always worth $1. Even if you leave your money in for 50 years, when you come back to redeem your shares each one will still be worth $1.

Of course, the fund would have been paying an amount on your investment the whole time, which you could have automatically reinvested into the fund or received in the form of a check. The amount paid would change with current short-term interest rates. If you reinvested the interest, your account's overall value would increase, but the price of each individual share would still be $1.

Some money market funds are tax-free. They invest in short-term debt from various municipalities. If you buy shares from a tax-free fund that invests only in your state, you won't have to pay city, state, or federal tax.

International and Global

Funds that identify themselves as "international" invest only in foreign countries, while "global" funds invest in both foreign countries and in the United States. These funds cover all three of

the basic asset classes. Stocks, bonds, and even money market instruments are available from other countries. As for international and global mutual funds, those that concentrate on stocks are the most popular.

This section explains the reasons to consider international investing, looks at the special risks involved, and then presents the different kinds of international and global funds.

Reasons to Consider International Investing

As I see it, there are two primary reasons to consider international investing: the world market offers great opportunity, and international investing provides broad diversification. As you now know, diversification reduces risk and increases return.

The World Market Offers Great Opportunity

For a long time the United States dominated the world market. There was no need for U.S. investors to look overseas for places to put their money because all the action was right here at home. That isn't the case anymore. In the mid-1960s, U.S. stocks accounted for more than 70 percent of the world market. By the mid-1980s that number dropped to only 50 percent, and by 1988 the U.S. world market share stood at 29 percent. It has fluctuated since then, but the chances of it ever dominating the market again are slim.

Established Markets This is important because it means that most of the world's investment opportunities lie outside our country. If you restrict yourself to U.S. investments, you are missing out on some of the best companies in the world. For example, imagine two funds that want to invest in the automobile industry. The first fund only buys U.S. stocks, so its choices are Ford, General Motors, and Chrysler. The second fund buys stocks anywhere in the world, so its choices include all the U.S. companies plus Toyota, BMW, Volkswagen, Nissan, and many others. Which fund do you think captures the true opportunity of the auto industry? The second one, of course. It has all the choices of the first fund plus many more. Put simply, global funds enjoy the freedom to pursue investment opportunity wherever it exists.

That freedom is a valuable one too. According to Morgan Stanley Capital International, the annual compound rate of return, including dividends, for the U.S. stock market from 1976 to 1991 was 13.8 percent. That looks good until you see that during the same 15-year period the United Kingdom returned 19.4 percent, Sweden returned 19.2 percent, France returned 17.8 percent, and Japan and Hong Kong each returned 17.5 percent.

If you invested $1,000 in a fund that returned the U.S. figure of 13.8 percent over that time period, you would have had $6,952 in 1991. If you had placed $1,000 in a fund that returned the United Kingdom's 19.4 percent over that time period, you would have had $14,291 in 1991. International investing would have paid you an additional $7,339! Of course, this example compares the U.S. return to the highest national return, which most international funds won't match. Nonetheless, you can see how much opportunity the world market holds.

Emerging Markets The world economy continues to grow as poor countries build infrastructures and take advantage of modern communication to trade with established countries. The U.S. economy has reached a level of maturity that makes it difficult for it to keep pace with these emerging markets.

Areas like Latin America, Southeast Asia, Eastern Europe, and Africa are building economic foundations. Their growth is at times astounding. At other times they stumble and leave investors dizzy with losses. Over time, however, these emerging markets will reach a mature posture, and those investors who've ridden the steady rise will be richer for it. On page 23 you learned about using standard deviation to gauge the volatility of different mutual funds. Markets use the standard deviation measurement just like mutual funds, and it looks at the same thing: the percentage amount that the market's annual return differs from its average return.

While the S&P 500 had a standard deviation of about 18 percent from 1984 to 1994, Mexico's standard deviation was 70 percent and Turkey's was over 125 percent. In 1990, the U.S. lost 6 percent, but the Philippines lost 54 percent. No doubt about it: emerging markets are a risky proposition.

Remember, though, that with all investments risk brings reward over time. In 1993, the U.S. gained 11 percent, but the Philippines gained 134 percent. Emerging markets might be way down one year and way up the next, but over time their numbers should average out to a healthy return.

International Investing Provides Broad Diversification

On page 4 you learned that mutual funds make it easy to spread your money among different investments. On page 25 you learned about the importance of allocating your money among the three basic asset classes: stocks, bonds, and the money market to achieve even further diversification. Finally, you spent time on page 28 considering what percentage of your long-term goal portfolio should be allocated to international investments. Now you'll learn the value of investing your money across different countries to achieve the broadest diversification possible.

In the same way that it's important to own more than one company's stock in case that company performs poorly, it's important to invest in more than one country's economy in case that country performs poorly. For U.S. investors, "that country" is probably the United States because while people from other countries are accustomed to investing overseas, we are not yet.

The U.S. economy and the world economy do not correlate. That means that when the U.S. is booming, other parts of the world might be in a recession, and when other parts of the world are making money hand over fist, the U.S. might be going through hard times. This non-correlation means that investing internationally can smooth out the year-to-year returns of your portfolio and, at the same time, give you higher overall returns than you would have with a purely U.S. portfolio of investments. That's the best of all worlds or, in this case, the best of all countries.

This is a key point: making international investments part of your long-term portfolio reduces your risk and increases your return. Want proof?

Look at the following chart. It shows the results of research done by Ibbotson Associates of Chicago, revealing that international investing helps a portfolio. The dark bars on the left show each portfolio's volatility, or daily price fluctuations. The light bars on the right show each portfolio return. Notice that the portfolio in the middle, which is a mixture of 40 percent U.S. stocks and 60 percent foreign stocks, fluctuated less and returned more than the portfolio on the left, which is 100 percent U.S. stock.

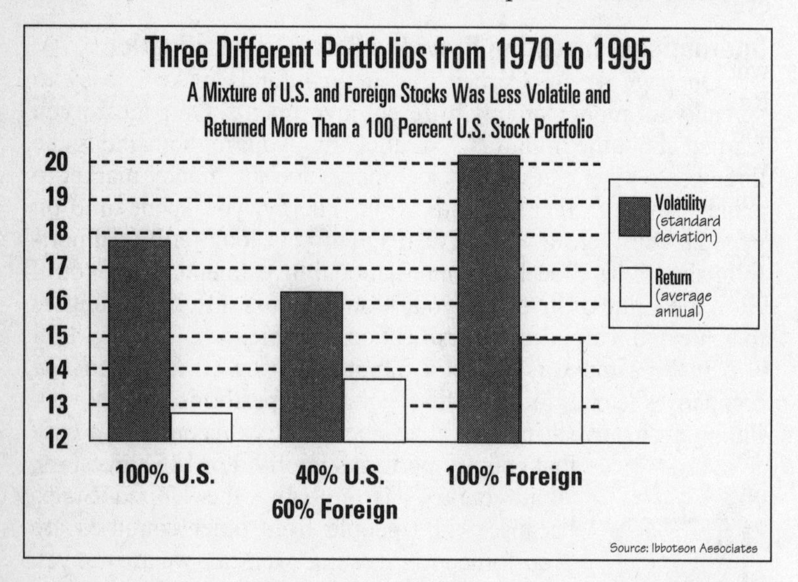

As the chart shows, international investing makes a lot of sense for the long term. It's a great way to diversify your portfolio and allows you to take advantage of the non-correlation between U.S. and international markets. When the U.S. is faltering, your portfolio can reap the benefits of healthy investments overseas. You decrease your risk and increase your return when you make international investments part of your long-term portfolio.

Special Risks of International Investing

While the reasons to consider international investing are compelling, you should be aware of two special risks: political instability and currency fluctuations.

Political Instability

It's hard enough to keep abreast of the U.S. political scene. How would you like to monitor other political systems as well? That's exactly what international and global fund managers do every day.

Political instability is of most concern in emerging markets, where "government" might mean the guy with the most guns. Revolutions wreak havoc on economies. You never know when a social uprising will topple the current government and take the value of your investments down with it. Even a challenge to the government can cause trouble. For example, when the government of Sri Lanka stopped negotiations with rebel Tamils in May 1995, investors braced themselves for a slow tourist season with repercussions extending to the rest of the economy. To make matters worse for investors, the Sri Lankan government showed signs of siding with labor unions to increase standard wages. Paying workers more would mean a smaller bottom line for companies and a lower stock value for investors.

It doesn't always take a revolution to harm international investments. Established countries change leaders on a regular basis, and new policies can greatly affect the investment climate.

Currency Fluctuations

The value of the U.S. dollar changes with regard to other national currencies. This fluctuation can leave an otherwise unchanged investment worth more or less than it was worth before the fluctuation.

For example, a fund that invests in Japan buys stock that is priced in yen, not dollars. If the value of that stock increases, investors should be wealthier for it. But what if the conversion from yen to dollars decreases the value of the investment? It's possible to lose money on a rising foreign stock.

Think about it. If the Japanese stock rises 20 percent but the yen falls 30 percent compared to the dollar, you would have an overall loss of 10 percent. On the other hand, currency fluctuations can work to your benefit. If the Japanese stock falls 20 percent and the yen rises 30 percent, you would see an overall gain of 10 percent even though your investment lost value. If the stock rises 20 percent and the yen rises 30 percent, your investment would go through the roof!

Different Kinds of International and Global Funds

Now that you've read how great it is to invest overseas, you're probably wondering what mutual funds have to offer in this area. Plenty. The hundreds of funds available that invest overseas fall into four categories: global, international, emerging market, and regional. Each category is explained below.

Global

These funds invest their money both in the United States and abroad. They are a good way to achieve international allocation if you are just starting out and don't have much money to invest. They are less volatile than funds pursuing 100 percent foreign investment, and can take advantage of good economic climates wherever they occur.

A definite advantage to investing in a global fund is that an investment professional is deciding what percentage to allocate overseas. The fund manager examines market trends from around the world before investing the fund's money. He or she isn't limited to a single country.

Funds that aren't necessarily grouped under the "global" heading in mutual fund listings might still be global. For example, the Janus fund is considered a growth fund but allocates about 15 percent of its assets to foreign investments. The distinction between funds grouped under the global heading and other funds that purchase foreign investments is that the global funds usually hold a larger percentage of foreign investments. For example, Templeton World is a global fund, and it allocates about 45 percent of its assets overseas.

International

International funds allocate all of their money to foreign investments. They diversify across many different economies and continents. An international fund might place 50 percent of its money in Europe, 30 percent of it in Asia, 10 percent in Latin America, and the remaining 10 percent in South America.

These funds are a good way for you to take international diversification into your own hands. Instead of relying on a global fund to allocate a percentage of assets overseas, using an international fund allows you to choose exactly how much of your money is invested outside the United States. If you decide that you want one-fifth of your portfolio overseas, you can place exactly that amount in an international fund and put the rest in other funds that invest only in the United States.

Because international funds tend to be broadly diversified, they are a safe way to invest overseas. They might fluctuate more than a U.S. fund, but remember that foreign markets and our market don't correlate. In a year when your U.S. funds are struggling, your international fund might be the one thing that keeps your overall return positive.

Emerging Market

Ignoring the established economies of the world, emerging market funds invest in fledgling economies that are just now building a foundation. These funds want to be the first to recognize companies that are scrambling to reach the top of their young markets.

You already know that it's best to buy a company's stock before the company reaches maturity. It would have been a thrill to buy Apple Computer stock back in 1982 when the personal computer was considered futuristic. Apple might still be a good buy, but its potential has already been largely realized. Now it's a mature, established company.

It works the same way with world markets. The United States, Japan, England, and France are mature and established.

There are opportunities within these established economies but, as a whole, they produce unspectacular returns. But emerging markets are like Apple Computer in 1982. They have more potential than history. They're trying to compete in the world economy and might one day be as solid as Japan or England. If so, now's the time to buy.

That's the philosophy of emerging market funds. They usually divide their assets among several emerging markets like Africa, Latin America, Eastern Europe, and Southeast Asia.

Emerging market funds can produce amazing returns and sickening losses in the same year. They are risky and should be seen as long-term investments that are just part of your overall portfolio.

Regional

These funds choose a region of the world or even a single country in which to invest all of their money. There are Latin American funds, Pacific Rim funds, Brazil funds, Canada funds, and hundreds of others.

The biggest advantage to regional funds is their narrow focus. That said, the biggest disadvantage to regional funds is also their narrow focus. It all comes down to the performance of the region in question. If you invested in a fund that targets Zimbabwe, you'd have been shaking your head in 1992, when the country's market lost 60 percent. All of your friends would have said they told you so. You might have been tempted to cut your losses and move what was left of your investment into a savings account. If instead you hung on for one more year, you could have visited your friends at the end of 1993, when the Zimbabwe market returned 144 percent. Now, that's sweet revenge.

Regional funds share many of the characteristics that you find in sector funds, which you read about on page 39. Sector funds target parts of the U.S. economy, and their entire performance depends on that sector. You might want to read about sector funds again to compare them with regional funds.

Other Kinds of Funds

This section covers funds that don't fit under a single objective. Some combine objectives and others focus on a method of investing instead of an objective.

Asset Allocation

These funds combine the strategies of all three basic fund objectives in a single fund. They can buy the stock of small and large companies, all types of bonds, and can keep a certain amount of their capital in the money market. Some even invest overseas. Like their name says, they allocate your money across different kinds of investments and enjoy a lot of room to maneuver. Asset allocation funds can put all of their money into stocks or none of it, all of it into bonds or none of it. The allocation is based on market conditions. These funds provide an easy way for investors to diversity.

You know that every mutual fund diversifies your money to a certain extent. For example, if you send $100 to a growth fund, it purchases the stock of many different large growth companies, not just a single company. But it won't, for the most part, purchase bonds or stock from small upstart companies, or money market instruments. In an allocation fund, $100 buys investments from each of the three major asset classes. The goal is for the fund manager to allocate your money in a way that is most appropriate for the current economic climate. Thus, when the stock market is soaring, you would expect an asset allocation fund to own more stocks than bonds. If Wall Street is going down in flames, an asset allocation fund should move most of its money into bonds and the money market.

Asset Allocation Funds Combine All Three Objectives

Allocation funds are best for investors with medium-term goals. While they are riskier than the money market and therefore provide a higher rate of return, they are not as risky as growth funds and should lose less money when stocks drop. Thus, allocation funds are good for medium-term goals, which I define as anywhere from 6 to 10 years.

There are different flavors of allocation funds. Some tend to seek growth while others seek income. Fidelity Investments specifies in the names of its three allocation funds which tendency each one has. They are called Asset Manager, Asset Manager Growth, and Asset Manager Income. The income fund allocates most of its money to bonds, the growth fund allocates most of its money to stocks, while the core asset manager fund seeks a balanced allocation among all three asset classes. It's important that you understand what tendency an asset allocation fund embraces before you invest money in it.

Asset allocation funds are not the Shangri-La of the investment world. In theory, they should be all-weather funds because the manager can adjust the holdings to reflect market conditions. This hasn't always proven true in the past, however, and there's no guarantee that it will in the future. In its March 31, 1995, semi-annual report, the Fidelity Asset Manager Growth fund reported a -4.02 percent 6-month return and a -2.04 percent 12-month return. The fund manager explained that the fund had been heavily invested in Mexico when the value of the peso dropped, and held other foreign investments that didn't perform well. The fund became extra cautious after its poor showing in 1994 and returned only 20 percent in 1995, a year the S&P 500 returned 37 percent.

The lesson to learn is not that asset allocation funds are bad, but that most investments take time. An investor who needs his or her money in the next 6 or 12 months is gambling to place it in the Asset Manager Growth fund. The money is better served in a money market fund or a bank savings account. Those who kept their money in Asset Manager Growth since its start in 1991 achieved an average annual return of 11.39 percent as of March 31, 1995. The decent return is due in large part to the same foreign investments that caused the losses in 1994. All investments have their moments of glory and shame.

So you see, asset allocation funds require a medium-term time frame. They try their best to ride the current economic wave, but don't expect them to do it impeccably.

Balanced

Similar to asset allocation funds, balanced funds buy a mixture of investments from all three asset classes. The difference is that balanced funds don't have as much flexibility as allocation funds.

While an allocation fund can vary its concentration in any class from 100 percent to 0 percent, balanced funds usually limit themselves to a maximum stock concentration of 65 percent. Also, the kind of stocks that balanced funds tend to buy are those of established companies like General Electric and Exxon. Most balanced funds don't buy small company stocks, as an asset allocation fund could.

Considering these factors, balanced funds are generally more conservative investments than allocation funds. They try to adjust their investments with changing economic times, but can't guarantee anything. As with allocation funds, I recommend at least a medium-term time frame for balanced fund investments.

Index

An index fund's investments precisely reflect a market index, such as the S&P 500 (see text box "What Is an Index?" on page 60). It buys stock in all or many of the same companies that make up the index. The advantage to an index fund is that your return will mirror the index average—your return *is* the index average, minus fund expenses. The drawback is that you're guaranteed to never beat the index average. But, as you'll see, the majority of stock mutual funds don't beat the average anyway, and their expenses are usually higher than index fund expenses.

Index Funds Are a Great Choice for Most Investors

What Is an Index?

A bunch of stocks grouped together and monitored to see how they perform. An index is a profile of a market segment. It provides a point of reference to gauge the relative performance of different investments. There are indexes that measure large companies, small companies, international markets, and bonds.

You probably already use indexes in other parts of your life, although you might not know it. We create them all the time to help ourselves compare different values. For example, let's say you are interested in buying a new Dodge Neon. If one of your main selection criteria is fuel economy, how do you know if the Neon performs well in that area? You compare it's miles-per-gallon number to the average miles-per-gallon number of other midsize passenger cars, such as the Ford Escort and the Honda Accord. After several comparisons, you know what is a good number, what is average, and what is below average. Notice that you don't compare the Neon's MPG to that of a Geo Metro or a Chevy Suburban. Those vehicles are in different classes and are irrelevant to your comparison. Thus, in this case, midsize passenger cars make up your index.

An investment index that almost everyone knows is the Dow Jones Industrial Average. It averages the performance of 30 blue chip stocks but, since it's an average, doesn't adjust for the various sizes of the companies it tracks.

More useful to investors is Standard & Poor's 500 Stock Index (S&P 500). It tracks the 500 U.S. companies with the highest stock value, giving weight to those that are biggest. It accounts for 80 percent of the New York Stock Exchange.

For people investing in small companies, the Russell 2000 or Value Line Average would be more appropriate. Both track the performance of small companies.

Many investors feel that big company indexes like the Dow or S&P 500 don't reflect the market anymore. Lately there's been a move toward new indexes, such as the Russell 3000, that track a mixture of large and small companies in an effort to capture what the market is really like.

The ultimate index is the Wilshire 5000, which tracks every stock in the New York Stock Exchange (NYSE), the

American Stock Exchange (AMEX), and the National Association of Securities Dealers Automated Quotations (NASDAQ). In short, the entire stock market!

The Lehman Brothers Aggregate Bond Index tracks the bond market, and the Morgan Stanley Capital International Europe Australia Far East (EAFE) Index tracks about 1,100 foreign stocks in 20 countries.

There are dozens of indexes, and you'll see different ones used as you become more familiar with mutual funds. Just remember that each provides a standard performance number for comparison between different funds.

Index funds make sense for the long- or medium-term investor because the market has an upward trend over time. Plus, there is no skill involved in running an index fund because it automatically divides itself among the stocks of its index. Therefore, management costs are usually kept low.

Efficient Market Theory

The word *theory* in the heading makes this section look scary, but it isn't. An investment theory called the Efficient Market Theory says that eventually all funds return to the market average. The reason is that all investors collectively own the stock market, and stocks are priced by what investors know. The theory states that the only thing driving a stock price higher than it should be is late-breaking, exclusive information and that the odds of ever receiving such information before everyone else are low. Once the information is used in the marketplace, it is no longer late-breaking or exclusive because the entire market reacts accordingly. Used investment secrets become public knowledge.

The theory's conclusion is that nobody *consistently* beats the market average. Certain fund managers might do it in a given year or even over a longer time period, but not forever.

Evidence in favor of the Efficient Market Theory abounds and, if anything, the theory is too kind because most funds return *less* than the market average. Over the past two decades both the S&P 500 and the Wilshire 5000 indexes outpaced the average stock mutual fund. In the February 1995 issue of *Money*, the magazine reported that out of 426 stock funds in service for at least ten years, only 92 had equaled or exceeded the 14.5 percent annualized return of the S&P 500. That's barely more than one-fifth of the funds. In 1994 specifically, all growth stock funds averaged together posted a loss of 1.6 percent while the S&P 500 posted a 1.3 percent gain. In 1995 the average stock fund returned 25 percent. Sounds great, right? Wrong. The S&P 500 cranked out 37 percent.

A "Passive" Investor

If you accept the Efficient Market Theory, then an index fund makes a lot of sense. Instead of fighting day after day for a big win only to end up either matching the market or losing to it, index investors "passively" accept market returns. Doing so allows them to achieve better results than their active counterparts, and with lower expenses.

Why do passive investors incur lower expenses? Because there is less trading involved in passive investing. Active investing, as its name implies, requires the active buying and selling of stocks as they come into and out of favor. All that trading generates commission expenses that a passive investor avoids. Plus, mutual fund managers in active funds require compensation for their efforts. On the other hand, computers can manage index mutual funds because all that's required is an equal distribution of fund assets across the index. It involves no interpretation, no market timing, and no Harvard MBA.

Some investors disagree with the Efficient Market Theory. They say that certain people have a knack for picking winning stocks. But even if you accept that as true, how can you be sure your fund manager is one of them? With more than 8,000 managers competing, the chances are slim.

Also, the market is a closed system. When someone wins, someone else eventually loses. If every stock always increased in value, everybody would win. But stocks don't always increase. When someone sells at a price peak, someone else buys at that peak. Since it's a price peak, both can't come out ahead.

Vanguard

It is impossible to discuss index funds without mentioning Vanguard, the second largest mutual fund company in the U.S.

and the industry's index evangelist. Large-company pension managers used index funds long before the general public knew about them. Then in 1976 Vanguard introduced index funds to individual investors and has led the industry with its breadth of offerings and the amount of index money under its management.

Vanguard is known for maintaining low expense ratios. One of its products is the "Index Trust," which is a group of six funds that each tracks a different U.S. stock index. The trust's expense ratios range from .18 percent to .20 percent while the average stock fund expense ratio is 1.27 percent. Vanguard also offers index funds for international stocks, U.S. bonds, and other categories.

Free Information

For a compelling look at index investing and more information about the Index Trust, call The Vanguard Group at 800–662–7447. Ask to receive the company's most current literature about indexing and an investment kit. In 1995 Vanguard offered a booklet called *The Triumph of Indexing*, which contained a 6-page look at how index funds have proven their critics wrong since 1976 and a 38-page overview of index fund investing in six categories: U.S. stocks, international stocks, U.S. bonds, a balanced investment program, a tax-managed investment program, and a lifetime investment program. Each category was discussed entirely with excerpts from former Vanguard Chairman John C. Bogle's 1994 Annual Report letters for six Vanguard index funds. Of course, all of the company's literature is Vanguard-centric. However, because Vanguard is the best indexer in the industry, consider the information's inward focus to be an advantage.

Life Cycle

Similar to asset allocation funds, life cycle funds spread investors' money across different asset classes. With one check you'll be buying stocks, bonds, and money market instruments.

The difference is that the mixture of assets changes with the investor's age. A young man would have most of his money in stocks, a middle-aged woman would convert some of her stock portfolio to bonds, and a retired couple would have almost everything in bonds and the money market.

In a life cycle fund, these adjustments across asset classes occur automatically as the investor ages. Because of their emphasis on time progression, life cycle funds are best for retirement accounts and other long-term goals. You don't want to put short-term money into a mutual fund that adjusts allocations as you get older.

Precious Metals

These funds buy a combination of the metals themselves, like gold and silver, and stock in the companies that mine and distribute the metals. There's nothing magical about precious metal; it's just another type of investment. However, expect returns to be sporadic and extreme. Gold funds, for example, have had years when the average return for all of them was 97 percent. Lexington Strategic has returned 265 percent in a single year, but it has also lost 61 percent in a year.

There are years when gold is worth huge sums of money and years when it's not, just like the rest of the investment scene. If you are attracted to the idea of owning it, a mutual fund is certainly safer than buying gold bullion. Precious metals are thought by many to be a guard against inflation because their value should rise along with it. But in recent years there hasn't been a correlation between inflation and the price of precious metals. In fact, precious metals don't follow any of the standard market indicators.

Why do people invest in precious metal funds? Some of the diversified mutual fund types, like asset allocation or life cycle, dedicate part of their portfolio to precious metal, but many do not. This is a section of the investment world that is often overlooked by general mutual funds. Therefore, if you want to further diversify your money, precious metals could be an option for you.

Remember that the returns from precious metals will be extreme. They focus on a small sector of the economy, and their results depend entirely on that sector. So treat precious metals funds like sector funds (page 39). Only invest when you already have a solid investment base in general funds such as growth or income. Precious metals fund investors should have a long-term time frame.

Social Conscience

Yes, it's true. There are politically correct mutual funds.

Some pride themselves in buying stock from companies that contribute to things like medicine, world peace, or environmental awareness. Others will not invest in companies that encourage activities such as smoking, drinking, pornography, or gambling. I like to call these the "happy funds."

It's getting harder to decide which funds are socially conscientious because the economy is interdependent. Should a happy fund invest in a railroad company that transports liquor? How about in a printing company that produces fliers for casinos? Or what about a major oil company that recycles its shipping containers? Some happy funds would and some would not. So if this is a consideration for you, you'll need to read the fund's prospectus for its special guidelines. You'll learn to read a prospectus on page 84.

4 Investing in the Right Funds

You've thought about your goals, decided on a time frame for each one, considered how much risk you're willing to take, and given thought to a good allocation among the three asset classes. You're also familiar with the different kinds of mutual funds. Now you're ready to start looking at specific funds for your goals.

This chapter shows how to match your allocation to fund categories, how to find the right funds, what to request from fund companies, how to select your funds, how to purchase your funds, and when and how to sell your funds.

Matching Your Allocation to Fund Categories

Once you've decided how you want to allocate your money for a certain goal, you're halfway to knowing where the money should go. You spent time deciding on an allocation for each of your goals in "What Allocation Is Right for You?" on page 29. Look over the allocations you chose. You wrote whether you are willing to accept high, medium, or low risk and decided on a mix of stocks, bonds, and money market instruments. Also, for your long-term goals, you considered allocating a percentage of your money to international investments. Now you'll take those decisions and apply to them to appropriate fund categories.

The Fund Categories

For a short-term goal, you might have chosen to place all of your money in the money market. For that, the choice is simple: select from different money market funds. For a medium-term goal, perhaps you chose a mixture of stocks, bonds, and the money market. To achieve your target mix, you could choose from among different growth, income, and money market funds or select a fund that combines all three asset classes such as an asset allocation fund or a balanced fund. For your long-term goals, you probably allocated most of your money to stocks, both domestic and international. For that, choose from different stock and international funds.

Compare your allocation choices to the different fund categories. Each category specializes in certain asset classes. Choose categories that match the allocation among asset classes that you want to achieve. To refresh your memory, here is the table of categories that you read on page 35:

Fund Category	Invests Primarily In	Best For
Growth	Large Company Stocks	Long-term or Medium-term
Aggressive Growth	Small Company Stocks	Long-term
Sector	Stocks from a Market Sector	Long-term
Income	Bonds and High-Dividend Stocks	Medium-term or Short-term
Growth and Income	Stocks and Bonds	Long-term or Medium-term
Money Market	Money Market Instruments	Short-term
International and Global	International and U.S. Securities	Long-term
Asset Allocation	All Asset Classes	Long-term or Medium-term
Balanced	All Asset Classes	Long-term or Medium-term
Index	Stocks or Bonds from an Index	Long-term or Medium-term
Life Cycle	All Asset Classes	Long-term
Precious Metals	Precious Metals and Related Stocks	Long-term
Social Conscience	"Responsible" Company Stocks	Long-term

For my Sport Coupe goal, I chose on page 29 to allocate 25 percent of my investment to stocks, 40 percent to bonds, and 35 percent to the money market. So I would probably select a growth fund, an income fund, and a money market fund or choose an asset allocation fund that seeks a balance between the three asset classes. Since this is a short-term goal and not a huge amount of money, the asset allocation fund would be simplest.

For a retirement account, however, I wouldn't choose the allocation fund. Since the retirement will grow to a large amount of money, it makes sense to spread it out among different funds altogether instead of concentrating in one fund that allocates among the three classes. Holding multiple funds magnifies the advantages that attract people to mutual funds to begin with, namely diversification and professional management. It's a good idea to have multiple managers, each handling a part of your money. That way if one makes a bad call, you still have the others pulling for you. Just how many managers? Glad you asked. The next section discusses the number of funds you should own.

How Many Funds to Own

Most households in the U.S. that invest in mutual funds only own one or two. That might be trouble if those one or two sink. Another problem is owning too many funds. If you own too many

stock funds, you are basically creating an index fund out of your stock portfolio. The reason is that each of the funds invests in a segment of the market, and there are only so many segments. When you invest in enough of them, you are targeting the whole stock market. If that's your goal, choose a total market index fund. It's cheaper than paying the expenses of five actively managed funds and achieves the same goal.

There is no ideal number of funds to own, but I can give you a range. Owning between three and eight funds makes sense. Owning at least three gives you good diversification to protect against a wayward fund. Stopping at eight keeps your portfolio from spreading too thin across the market and diluting good returns. With a mixture of eight funds, you could own two growth funds, two income funds, two money market funds, and two international funds. That's a well-diversified portfolio.

There's a problem with the three to eight range, however. You might not have enough money to afford the minimums on three funds. What should you do?

For short-term goals, owning a single money market fund is acceptable. It won't lose money, so you don't have to worry about risk. Plus, if you have emergency expenses and need to tap your investment account, a money market fund makes it easy to do so.

For medium- and long-term goals, start with an index fund. Because your goal is far away, you can tolerate short-term market fluctuations. An index fund guarantees that your single investment is diversified, you pay low expenses, and your returns reflect the performance of an entire market instead of a few investments. See page 59 for a complete description of index funds.

If you can afford to own more than one fund in pursuit of your goals, decide on a number that can provide you with the allocation you chose earlier.

Researching the Right Funds

You know what allocations are right for your goals, and you've matched those allocations to fund categories, such as growth or income. Now you need to decide which specific funds will get your money. You'll decide after doing research. This section explains the information you need and then shows where to find it.

Take this guidebook and a photocopy of the Mutual Fund Information Sheet located in the back along with you as you do research. The information sheet looks like this:

Fund Name and Phone	3-Year	5-Year	10-Year	Relative Rating	Beta	Alpha	R-Squared	Standard Deviation

Initial Invest	Loads	Expense Ratio	Fund Size	Manager Since	Portfolio Turnover

Fill in the sheet as you find information.

The Information You Need

Related information is grouped together on your information sheet. This section explains each piece of information, except fund name and phone. I'm guessing you're all over that one.

Past Performance

1. Look at the Fund's Performance

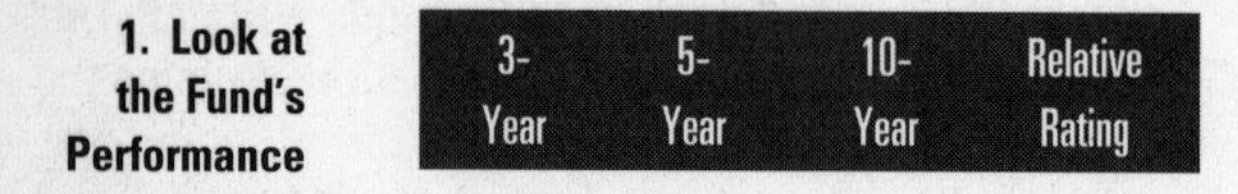

3-Year	5-Year	10-Year	Relative Rating

The phrase you'll see most often around mutual fund literature is "past performance is no guarantee of future results."

That's true, but most of us would prefer investing in a fund that has historically done well than in one that has never made money. You should be most concerned with how a fund performed in the past 3-, 5-, and 10-year time periods.

With Performance, a Bigger Number Is Better

The 3-year average annual return gives you an idea of how the fund has done in recent years, and the 5-year shows a bit of history. The 10-year gives you an idea of how the fund's strategy is working over time. A 1-year return is nice to know but doesn't reveal as much as the longer time frames because anybody can get lucky or hit a pothole.

Also, look over the *relative* performance of each fund. It's good to know how it did overall but better to see how it did relative to its peer group. If the fund that interests you returned an average of 12 percent for the past three years, you might be smiling. But that's not so hot if every other fund of that kind returned 18 percent during the same period.

Different sources provide a relative rating in different formats. Some rank funds by decile so you can see if your fund placed in the top 10 percent, middle 10 percent, second-to-lowest 10 percent, and so on. Others rank funds by quartile so you can see if your fund fell into the top 25 percent, bottom 25 percent, or somewhere in between. Still others provide grades from A to E, where those receiving an A were in the top 20 percent and those receiving an E were in the bottom 20 percent.

Whichever relative rating system you find is fine. Be sure that you understand whether the relative rating is against other funds like the one you're interested in or against all funds. For example, a technology sector fund might have performed terribly compared to other technology funds, but great compared to all funds in general.

What's a Good Performance?

It's different for each type of mutual fund. In a year when the stock market is soaring, you expect stock funds to do well. In down years you expect stock funds to do poorly. Remember from page 25 that the return for stocks has been 10.3 percent, bonds 5 percent, and money market 3.7 percent.

The best way to gauge whether a fund has kept pace with the market is by comparing it to a market index, such as the S&P 500. If a fund consistently underperforms its index, you'd be better off investing in an index fund which returns exactly what the index returns, minus small expenses. Also, pay attention to how a fund does against its peers.

The bottom line is that you should never look at a fund's return by itself. Absolute numbers are meaningless. For example, does a 25 percent annual return sound good? You bet, and that's exactly what the average stock fund reported as its 1995 return. But guess what the S&P 500 returned that year? 37 percent. So, never lose sight of the market or a fund's peers.

Beta, Alpha, R-Squared, and Standard Deviation

2. Look at the Fund's Risk

Beta | Alpha | R-Squared | Standard Deviation

Next you'll gather risk measurements. The measurements are beta, alpha, R-squared, and standard deviation.

Beta First look at beta. Remember that market indexes have a beta of 1. If the fund's beta is greater than 1, the fund is more volatile than its index; if the fund's beta is less than 1, the fund is less volatile than its index. For a complete description of beta, see page 20.

Alpha Next write down the alpha. An alpha of 0 means the fund performed as expected for the risks it took. Positive numbers mean it did better than expected, and negative numbers mean it did worse. For a complete description of alpha, see page 21.

R-Squared Now find R-squared. A rating of 100 means that the fund's performance is attributed entirely to the behavior of its market index. A rating of 0 means that the fund's investments are different enough from its index that its performance is likely to be different too. Also, a low R-squared means the fund's beta is less reliable because beta compares the volatility of the fund to the volatility of the fund's index. If the fund doesn't follow its index, the beta comparison is meaningless. For a complete description of R-squared, see page 22.

Standard Deviation Last, write down the fund's standard deviation. This number is the range limit within which the fund's annual return has deviated from its own average return 67 percent of the time. So a fund with a standard deviation of 5 and an average annual return of 10 percent has posted returns between 5 percent and 15 percent during 67 percent of its history. A higher number indicates a more volatile fund. For a complete description of standard deviation, see page 23.

None of these four measurements is the last word, but together they indicate a fund's personality.

Costs

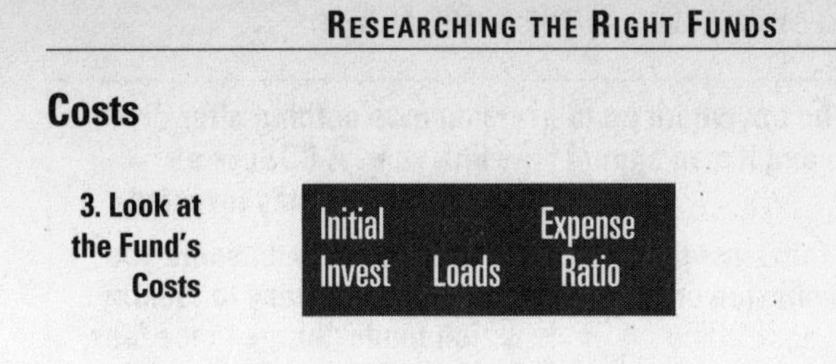

The following are costs associated with a mutual fund. They're important to you because a fund with lower expenses allows more of your investment money to work for you.

Initial Investment You need to know what the minimum initial investment is. It doesn't help to get your heart set on a fund and find out later that it only accepts initial investments of $25,000 when you were hoping to start a $500 nest egg toward your retirement.

With Costs, a Smaller Number Is Better

Loads Don't forget that some funds charge a commission. Watch out for loads and redemption fees. I recommend that you limit your search to no-load funds because they have done as well as their load counterparts. Same goes for those that charge redemption fees.

To illustrate how damaging loads can be, pretend you invested $1,000 in each of two funds. They both return average annual returns of 10 percent, but one charges a 5 percent load. After fifteen years your investment in the no-load fund would be worth $4,177, but in the load fund it would only be worth $3,968. The 5 percent load would have cost you $209. That might not seem like much compared to the nearly $4,000 your money would have become, but consider that it's equal to 21 percent of your initial investment.

Just When You Thought It Was Safe

There are a number of ways for a fund to take your money besides a load. The main ones are:

- **12b-1 fees. Named after the section of a ruling from the U.S. Securities and Exchange Commission that allows funds to charge investors for marketing expenses. The**

amount can be anywhere up to 1.25 percent, and it's an annual fee.

- **Redemption fees. Instead of taking a commission on your initial investment, some funds take it on the amount you withdraw. Some do both.**
- **Contingent deferred sales load (CDSL). A fee charged if investors withdraw their money before a specified duration of time. The amount charged decreases by a percentage each year up to the end of the duration, after which time no fee is charged. For example, a 5-percent CDSL over 5 years could cost you 5 percent if you redeem your shares within the first year, 4 percent within the second year, and so on until you owe nothing after the fifth year. A CDSL is an incentive to stay invested.**

None of this should scare you very much. It's easy to identify which funds charge these fees, and you can decide then if you want to invest. All costs are detailed on the fund prospectus, which you'll learn about on page 84.

I recommend choosing from funds that do not assess 12b-1 fees whenever possible. But a lot of funds do charge the 12b-1, and to rule all of them out would severely limit your options.

As for loads, redemption fees, and CDSLs, rarely pay them. There are too many good funds that don't charge these fees to justify investing in those that do.

Expenses Mutual fund companies aren't in this business for fun. They need to make a profit, and the way they do so is by charging shareholders an expense fee. This expense is in addition to any loads that a fund charges, and it is drawn from investment accounts on an annual basis.

High Expenses Make for an Unhealthy Investment

Expenses are expressed as a ratio of the expense to the fund's assets. Average for all mutual funds is around 1.00 percent, for stock funds it's 1.27 percent, and for bond funds it's .73 percent. International and sector funds tend to be more expensive in all categories.

The effect of the expense ratio is easy to calculate. Simply multiply your investment assets by the ratio to find what you'll pay each year. For example, if the fund has an expense ratio of 1.22 percent and you have $100 to invest, you'll pay $1.22 in expenses by the end of the year. Funds are required to show the calculations for you in the fund prospectus. You'll learn more about that on page 84.

Annual expenses are a direct drain on your return. That means that if your fund returns 10 percent in a given year but has a 1 percent annual expense, you only gain 9 percent.

That's 10 percent of your profits eaten by expenses! You might be tempted to think that a mere 1 percent can't make a difference, but it can. Consider two funds that both return 10 percent a year for fifteen years. One fund has an expense ratio of 1 percent, and the other has an expense ratio of 2 percent. Let's say you invest $1,000 in each fund. At the end of the fifteen years your investment in the 1 percent expense fund would be worth $3,642. In the 2 percent expense fund, it would only be worth $3,172. That extra 1 percent cost you $470!

Here's another thing to keep in mind: the annual expense is a guaranteed number, but the fund's return is not. That means that a low expense is a sure thing. Obviously funds try to get the highest return possible, and some claim that they're more expensive because of the quality of their management. But while quality stock picking isn't reliable, a low expense ratio is. This is the main argument in favor of index funds (see page 59). They have both a guaranteed return that matches their market index and a guaranteed low expense.

When choosing between similar funds that share an objective, selecting the one with a lower expense ratio makes sense. In effect, you are increasing your returns without increasing risk. That's a very difficult feat in investing, but low expenses are one way of accomplishing it. Keeping the annual expense low is an important consideration.

Bond Funds Need Especially Low Expenses

Low expenses are important to all investors, but they are vital to bond fund investors. The reason is that bond investing is more an exercise in mathematics than in judgment. It takes a certain intuition to choose which stocks are going to rise and what the future holds for specific companies. But since bonds have fixed face values and coupon rates, all it takes is a calculator and an idea of where interest rates are headed to make a good choice. So there are basically two ways to increase a bond fund's return: keep its expense ratio low or buy risky bonds. Most investors prefer the low expense ratio.

Size of the Fund

4. Look at the Fund's Size

Glance at how much money the fund is currently handling. It can make a difference if a fund manager is juggling $10 billion rather than $100 million. Occasionally certain funds do well in a given year and attract droves of new investors. Sometimes this overwhelms the fund manager as the amount of money under his or her control swells. Usually, however, any strain is temporary. After all, successful funds expect to grow.

There appears to be no correlation between the size and quality of a fund. The best funds in the industry come in all sizes, and they all started small. However, fund managers have said in interviews that there are times when having too much money makes it difficult to purchase the stock of smaller companies that they want to buy. They simply have too much money to spend and can't move it in and out of securities as quickly as smaller funds can.

While a fund's size isn't the most important factor, it can be influential. It's nice to know whether your money is part of a fund that can literally move the whole market when it buys and sells, or part of a fund that needs your money to afford an even number of shares.

The Fund Manager

5. Look at the Fund's Manager

You want an experienced fund manager. Many mutual fund advisers stress that the manager is the most important factor in deciding whether to invest in a particular fund. In interviews, most mutual fund managers themselves say that the biggest strength in managing money is experience.

With the Fund Manager More Experience Is Better

This makes sense because everything else is subjective. It's difficult to rate a person's intelligence or the quality of their judgment without a historical perspective. But a manager that has been with the same fund for a period of time can be rated quite easily. The fund's record is the manager's record and vice versa. The manager is as good as his or her results.

If the current fund manager has been in charge only since sunrise, then the fund's historic returns aren't very valuable. They will tell you how the fund's philosophy did but nothing about the person calling the shots. Instead, you would like to know the manager's history so you can at least see if he or she has performed well elsewhere.

Treat new managers like new brain surgeons. Let them get their training on somebody else.

Portfolio Turnover Rate

6. Look at the Portfolio Turnover

This number is expressed as a percentage of the entire fund portfolio value, which is all the stocks, bonds, and money market instruments the fund owns.

For example, if the portfolio turnover rate is 100 percent for a given year, that means the fund bought and sold enough securities to equal its total assets. If the rate is 275 percent, the fund bought and sold securities worth almost three times its total value. For a fund with $100 million in assets, that's $275 million worth of securities traded.

With Turnover Rate a Smaller Number Is Better

The portfolio turnover rate is helpful for tax considerations. The more a fund buys and sells assets, the greater the chance that it will have to distribute a capital gain to shareholders who will pay tax on the distribution. You'll read a complete discussion of capital gain distributions on page 110.

Portfolio turnover rate also helps estimate brokerage fees. A manager who buys and sells frequently racks up higher brokerage fees from the activity. The extra fees diminish the fund's return.

Where to Find the Information

Now that you know what information to look for, you need to know where to find it. This section tells you.

Magazines

A good place to start is the magazine rack at a local bookstore. There are hundreds of publications for investors, but you can stick with the better-known ones like *SmartMoney, Worth,* and *Kiplinger's*. See if there's a cover story that catches your eye—maybe one addresses your goals. If one of the magazines is doing an annual survey of mutual funds, buy it. It will be helpful for you to have that information when homing in on the right fund. Fund surveys are usually published in the first and third quarters of every year. Avoid the more complicated newspapers when you're beginning. You don't need detailed information contained in The *Wall Street Journal* or *Barron's* yet.

As you page through the magazines, pay attention to the ads you see for different mutual funds. Well-known companies like Fidelity, Invesco, Janus, T. Rowe Price, and Vanguard present information about their offerings. They show the past performance of certain funds and encourage you to call for a prospectus. Since the SEC monitors advertising, the information you get is reliable. Later, you'll find details not contained in the ads. If a fund grabs your attention because it seems to fit your needs, make note of its name and phone number on your information sheet.

Never forget that you're looking at advertising. Mutual fund companies want you to invest in their funds just as Heinz wants you to put its ketchup on your hamburgers. However, some of the fund advertisements are thoughtfully presented and can educate you as they present their goods. One of the best fund ads was run by Twentieth Century in the summer of 1995. The headline read:

One of Our Funds Just Gained Over 20% in One Year.

{But That's No Reason to Buy It.}

The ad explained: "After all, 1-year returns aren't what Twentieth Century is all about. Our perspective is long-term. The stocks in Twentieth Century's mutual funds are chosen primarily because they're considered to have better-than-average prospects for appreciation. And appreciation takes time. You'll see that some of our funds didn't exactly take your breath away during the latest 12-month period. And that's our point. In order to put the power of the stock market on your side, it's best to focus on long-term results." Whether readers chose to invest with Twentieth Century or not, the ad taught a valuable lesson.

Whatever you do, don't get excited over last year's big winners. Twentieth Century was right: that's no reason to buy a fund. Too many magazines create hoopla about funds that topped the 1-year return charts. Who cares? If you had invested in the fund a year ago, it would be nice to know that you lead the pack. But if you're doing research to find a good fund for your money, a 1-year return is meaningless. It doesn't tell you anything about the fund's strategy over time or about the manager's skill. Anybody can get lucky. That doesn't mean you should automatically ignore last year's winners. It's possible that the fund with the best 1-year return also has the best 3-year, 5-year, and 10-year returns among its peers. The point here is that you should never buy a fund just because it was one of last year's big winners.

Library Tools

After spending time with the magazines, take a trip to your local library. There you will find a host of research tools at your disposal, three that I want to highlight: *The Handbook for No-Load Fund Investors* by Sheldon Jacobs, *Morningstar Mutual Funds,* and *The Value Line Mutual Fund Survey*. Each is a collection of information about every fund that would interest you, and the Morningstar and Value Line publications are good places to find beta, alpha, R-squared, and standard deviation. Each of these three sources presents information in concise, standardized formats that make it easy for you to compare one fund to another. *The Handbook* is a single-volume reference with a fair amount of information while Morningstar and Value Line produce multi-volume references with comprehensive coverage.

Libraries have Lots of Fund Information

I recommend narrowing your fund list with *The Handbook* and getting complete information on the remaining funds from either Morningstar or Value Line. You can photocopy the comprehensive data on your finalists to take home with you. Then if you have questions as you look over your worksheet you can refer to the photocopies.

The Handbook for No-Load Fund Investors As an early screening device it's hard to beat *The Handbook for No-Load Fund Investors* by Sheldon Jacobs. This publication provides an honest discussion of the pitfalls and rewards of mutual fund investing followed by lists of fund information. You can use it to quickly eliminate certain funds from your list.

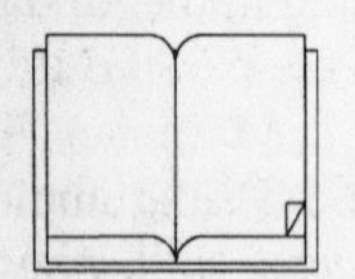

A Good Way to Narrow Your Choices

If, for example, you come to the library with a large group of funds to consider, *The Handbook* can whittle the number down to a select few based on your key requirements. You might quickly discover that some funds are closed to new investors, have a higher expense ratio than you want to pay, or don't have a high enough return for your liking. *The Handbook* reveals these facts much faster than Morningstar or Value Line. Once your list is reduced to a manageable size, you can turn to the big reference systems for complete information.

Morningstar Mutual Funds Morningstar's approach is to provide just about everything you could ever want to know about a fund in a single-page summary. To find particular funds, you must consult an index that ships every two weeks with a funds update. In a separate volume Morningstar includes a manual explaining the layout of its fund pages and what the different information means. I suggest you locate a fund's information page and start looking at it before you consult the manual. Much of the data is self-explanatory, and there's no use bogging down in the manual before you know if it's necessary.

A Comprehensive Reference System

Morningstar is best known for its star rating system, which assigns a fund 1 to 5 stars based on its past balance of risk and reward. To determine the monthly rating, Morningstar subtracts the fund's risk score from its return score and plots the resulting number along a bell curve with other funds of its kind. After an entire class of funds is plotted, the top 10 percent get 5 stars, the next 22.5 percent get 4 stars, the middle 35 percent get 3 stars, the next 22.5 percent get 2 stars, and the lowest 10 percent get 1 star.

The five-star rating is a widely cited claim in fund advertising despite the fact that it isn't foolproof. Morningstar intends for the star-rating system to reflect how well the fund has performed given the risks it took—not to predict future performance. In its manual Morningstar says that there might be times in a diversified portfolio of mutual funds that an investor would want to hold a 1-star or 2-star fund because such funds can often come from special categories that are currently doing poorly. The example Morningstar gives is the benefit of owning a gold fund even when every choice is rated 1 star. Even though gold funds are not doing well at that time, they are still a good hedge against inflation and might be appropriate as part of an overall investment strategy.

Another thing to know about the star rating is that it's calculated monthly. Funds will continue to advertise having earned a 5-star rating long after they've been downgraded. Finally, the stars hold no predictive value. They are only an after-the-fact look at how a fund balanced risk and reward.

None of this is to say that the star is worthless. It's actually quite helpful in narrowing down the list of potential funds that you want to own. Just remember that the stars are not foolproof and that they are intended as an initial screen only. To get the complete picture, look at the rest of Morningstar's data.

For information about subscribing to Morningstar products, see page 103.

The Value Line Mutual Fund Survey Value Line's reference is so similar to Morningstar's that once you know how to use one, you know how to use the other. Value Line also ships biweekly updates with indexes and also packs each fund's complete information onto a single page.

Another Comprehensive Reference System

Instead of the star-rating system used by Morningstar, Value Line ranks funds from 1 to 5 based on their performance and risk. A rank of 1 indicates the most return from the least amount of risk, and a rank of 5 indicates the least return from the most amount of risk. Value Line also includes a separate ranking that only measures risk by ranking funds from 1 to 5, where 1 indicates the least risky funds. The ranking is intended only as a screening device, just like the star system used by Morningstar.

A Value Line fund page shows all the information you would expect, such as past returns, expenses, and a description of the fund's management style. It also includes a calculation for how much $10,000 invested in the fund has done over several time periods and even reveals the effect of adding an additional $100 per month to the fund over the same time periods. Remember from page 32 that this strategy is called dollar-cost averaging and allows investors to buy more shares when the price is low and fewer shares when it's high, thereby reducing the average price paid per share. I highly recommend it, and Value Line does a great service by analyzing the effect of dollar-cost averaging in every mutual fund. You can see exactly how price volatility would have affected a regular investment program.

Value Line's biweekly ratings are kept in binders. A separate manual explains how to use the information and also includes a good overview of mutual fund investing. As with Morningstar, you don't need to consult the manual unless you have a question. Most of the information is self-explanatory.

For information about subscribing to Value Line products, see page 103.

Contacting the Funds for More Information

After your time with the magazines and the library, you will have narrowed your list of potential funds to a handful. The handful should be the most suitable to your needs judging from the information on the sheet you filled out.

Fund Company Phone Representatives Are Among the Best Anywhere

Now you need details, and they are available from mutual fund companies themselves. Each fund company has a toll-free number that you can call for more information or to speak with a representative. The phone representatives are well informed about their products and about mutual fund investing in general. Many are registered with the SEC and receive daily news summaries and updated fact sheets which they can share with you. Mutual fund company phone personnel provide some of the best customer service anywhere.

The detailed information you need at this point in your research comes in the form of a prospectus. A prospectus is a formal document that describes the fund's investment practices, expenses, risk involved, and other matters important to potential investors. The SEC requires all funds to reveal the same information in a standard format to make it easy for you to compare funds.

Call each fund company's 800 number and ask to receive a new investor's kit for the fund you're interested in. The company knows that you need a prospectus and will include one in the kit. Also ask to receive the latest annual report. You'll probably get brochures and possibly excerpts from magazine articles along with the kit that you request. Read everything, but concentrate on the prospectus and annual report.

The Prospectus

The prospectus will remind you of reading the fine print on a new credit card or the underside of your favorite safety ladder. To save you from falling asleep, here are the most important parts.

The Cover Page and Synopsis

You Must Always Read the Fund Prospectus Before Investing

The cover page and synopsis tell you the name of the fund, its investment objective, and the date of the prospectus. Make sure that you have the most current one. The SEC requires a fund to update its prospectus every 16 months.

Also verify basic facts like minimum initial investment amounts and highlight any special services such as check writing.

Fee Table

Inside you'll find a table containing all the costs involved with owning shares in the fund.

A completely no-load fund's shareholder transaction cost looks like this:

Maximum Sales Load on Purchases	None
Maximum Sales Load on Reinvested Dividends	None
Deferred Sales Charge	None
Exchange Fees	None
Annual Fund Operating Expenses	
Management Fee	0.78 %
12b-1 Fee	None
Other Expenses	0.39 %
Total Operating Expenses	1.17 %

The number amounts listed are different for every fund, but true no-loads print none in each category indicated. Remember, I recommend no-load funds.

The most important number for the long term is the bottom line: Total Operating Expenses. It tells you what percentage of your money you will be paying every year. The SEC requires funds to detail how these costs affect an investor redeeming shares after one, three, five, and ten years for an investment of $1,000 growing at 5 percent. This information comes after the expense chart and looks like this:

A shareholder would pay the following expenses on a $1,000 investment for the periods shown, assuming (1) a 5% annual return and (2) redemption at the end of each time period:

1 Year	3 Years	5 Years	10 Years
$12	$37	$65	$143

Since every prospectus is required to provide yearly expense information, it's easy for you to look among funds and see exactly how their expenses compare. Keep in mind that these annual expenses do *not* include up-front loads. That money is lopped off the top when you first invest.

Per-Share Data

Anything that looks like a tax table can't be all that appealing. Unfortunately, it's how the latest 10-year history of a fund's NAV is presented to you. It shows what a share was worth at the beginning of each year, calculates gains and losses for you, shows the share price at the end of the year, and gives you the total return as a percentage. Here's what a single year might look like:

Per-Share Data	Year Ended 1994
Net Asset Value—Beginning of Period	$7.39
INCOME FROM INVESTMENT OPERATIONS:	
Net Investment Income (Loss)	0.05
Net Gains or (Losses) on Securities	1.64

LESS DISTRIBUTIONS:	
Dividends (from Net Investment Income)	0.05
Distributions (from Capital Gains)	0.53
TOTAL DISTRIBUTIONS	0.58
Net Asset Value—End of Period	$8.50
TOTAL RETURN (%)	23.11
RATIOS:	
Net Assets—End of Period ($000 omitted)	$231,100

The Annual Report

The prospectus is dry reading, but the report will be a little easier on you. Funds are required to produce an annual report, and some provide semiannual and quarterly reports too. The main things that a report gives you over the prospectus is a look at performance over ten years, management's overview of how the fund invests, and a snapshot of the fund's current holdings.

Ten-Year Return Graph

This shows you what a $10,000 investment has done over 10 years. It is compared to an appropriate index, like the S&P 500 or Russell 3000. Since you can view the fund's progress through each year, you'll be able to see trends. You might discover that all returns have been mediocre except for one year that the fund returned 80 percent. That flash-in-the-pan stroke of luck could have boosted the fund's average annual return to 15 percent, for example, but you probably shouldn't choose the fund over a peer that has returned a steady 15 percent.

The graph takes into account all expenses. So if there's an 8.5 percent load for a fund, the graph starts out at $9,150 to reflect the charge.

Management Overview

The fund manager writes about what strategies he or she has implemented and discusses the result. The honesty in these overviews ranges from outstanding to shady. Everything is legal, of course, and nobody lies outright. But occasionally a manager phrases things in a meaningless way, as in "will continue seeking

Fund Manager After a Good Year

companies with upside potential." That's good to know, but you could assume as much. How many investors would send money to a fund seeking companies with downside potential?

The better overviews get specific. For example, if a fund sold all of its biotechnology stock for fear of health care reform, it should say so. If it is making a slow move from transportation companies to computer manufacturers, it should explain its reasoning. A candid overview indicates that the manager has nothing to hide and will be honest with you in future communications.

Statement of Holdings

This is where you find out if the fund puts its money where it claims to in the prospectus. Managers sometimes have a lot of flexibility in choosing what to buy. The statement of holdings shows you what is happening now.

It also gives you an appreciation for how diversified your money really is when you invest in a mutual fund. You'll find pages of stocks, bonds, and money market instruments listed with their percentage of the fund's portfolio.

You might find proportions that startle you. Most funds don't place much more than 2 percent of their money in any single asset, but what if you discover that a certain growth fund places 15 percent of its assets in one company's stock? If you think that company has a bright future, perhaps you should invest. On the other hand, it might be too focused for your tastes.

In most cases you'll look over a long list of household names in balanced proportions and simply "check off" that you looked at the fund's holdings. If the objective fits and the other measurements you've found in your research are good, don't sweat the details of what the fund owns. That's what the manager is paid to do.

Selecting Your Funds

At this point, you're ready to sit down at a table with all of the information you've gathered and make selections. On page 68 you decided how many funds to own based on the amount of money you have to invest and your goals. Now you'll select that many funds from the candidates you found in your research. Have the following items with you:

1. Your filled-out Mutual Fund Information Sheet.
2. Any magazines that contain information you've used in your research.
3. Photocopies of pages from *Morningstar* or *Value Line* that profile your fund candidates.
4. Prospectuses and other literature from the funds themselves.

Begin with your information sheet. Eliminate funds that don't compete with others you have listed. Start with obvious categories like sales loads and performance figures. Is there a fund that has done worse than the others over all three time periods? If so, check to see if its beta, alpha, or R-squared numbers are good enough to keep it in the running. If it has been volatile, as indicated by either a high beta, a high standard deviation, or both, but has failed to return an amount that justifies the volatility, strike it from your list.

This interplay between the figures on your information sheet is an important consideration for you as you analyze your finalists. Don't isolate a single piece of information on your sheet and use it to determine which funds get your money.

Think of your sheet like the information on several new homes you're considering. One might have a better view, but another costs less. One is closer to your church, but another is built by a lake. One has a three-car garage, but one has a Jacuzzi. Is any single factor more important than another? It all depends on your preferences. It's the same way with funds you're considering. Performance is a prime consideration, but expenses are important too. Only you can look at the information you've gathered and decide which funds best fit your goals and your attitude toward money.

The magazines, photocopies from *Morningstar* and *Value Line*, and fund company literature are good to have on hand for clarification. Just in case there's a question that your information sheet doesn't answer, you can consult these other sources of information. Also, don't hesitate to call any of the funds' toll-free phone numbers with questions. The representatives will gladly answer anything they can.

Purchasing Your Funds

Congratulations! You've analyzed a lot, discovered a group of funds that's right for you, gathered prospectuses, and should feel confident about your final fund choices. All that remains is filling out the application and sending your money.

With your new investor's kit you should have received an account application. If not, call the company and have them send you one. Fill out all the basic stuff like your name and address.

On page 34 I discussed the possibility of making money three different ways: having the value of your investment grow, sending more money on a regular basis, and reinvesting any income you receive. You leave the first one up to the fund and specify the last two on the application, as described below.

Regular Investments

Most funds offer a program to make regular investments easy. If your fund is one of them, there will be a section on the application for you to establish *automatic* bank transfers. You simply tell the fund what regular time period to use (like monthly or quarterly), what day during each time period to transfer, and how much to transfer.

Next you'll have to provide banking information so the fund knows where to go for your money. There will be a section asking for specifics, and you should enclose a voided, unsigned check or deposit slip for the fund's reference.

The beauty of automatic transfer is that there's no hassle. You won't put off investing because the car broke down and you couldn't get to the bank. No matter what happens, your money will make it into your investment and start working for you right away. If you need to have the fund skip a regular transfer, simply call the fund company a few days in advance and request that it do so.

I highly recommend that you take advantage of regular investing. If you can factor it into your personal budget, it will help you reach your goals. You'll automatically be dollar-cost averaging, and you'll have to map your direction only one time. If you've chosen your funds carefully and figured what amount you need to save each month, you'll reach your target. Periodic checkups will still be in order, but the basic structure of your investment plan will be solid.

Reinvesting Distributions

A small section of the application asks how you want to handle distributions of income. When stocks in the fund's portfolio pay a dividend or turn a profit when sold, or the bonds and Treasuries pay interest, you're entitled to a certain amount of that income for each share of the fund you own. You can choose from three different ways to receive it:

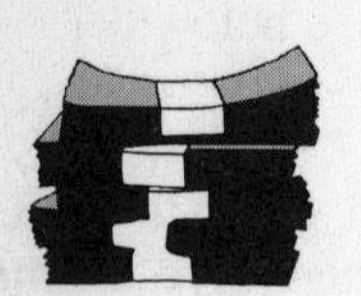

1. Have a check mailed to you.
2. Have all distributions reinvested in the fund. That means all the money you earn is used to buy more shares.
3. Have the distributions placed in a different fund with the same company, usually a money market fund.

Some fund companies encourage reinvestment by making it the default on the application. If you don't tell them otherwise, they'll reinvest your distributions. Reinvesting is a good way to help your investment grow. Why tempt yourself to spend by having a check mailed to you? Instead, have the distributions quietly placed back into the fund that created them.

When and How to Sell Your Funds

You will eventually sell your mutual funds to realize the profit or loss they've achieved. It could be that you've accomplished an investment goal or that one of your funds doesn't feel right anymore. How do you know when to sell? If you decide it's time to sell one of your funds, how do you do it? This section answers both questions: when to sell a fund and how to do it.

The next chapter, "Tracking Your Funds," shows ways to monitor your investments that can reveal if any of these selling conditions apply to one of your funds.

When to Sell a Fund

Here are four good times to consider selling a fund:

When You Reach Your Goal or Your Outlook Changes

It could come as a surprise that often it's not the mutual fund that causes a reason to sell, it's you. You might have invested in an aggressive growth fund early in the quest for a long-term goal. As you near the goal, the aggressive fund's volatility is no longer suitable to your time frame. It's prudent to reallocate, and that means selling the aggressive growth fund for a more conservative fund.

A similar situation occurs if you bought a fund for a specific purpose and it has already fulfilled that purpose or you're convinced that it never will. For example, say you thought the banking industry was poised for huge growth, so you invested in a banking sector fund two years ago. The banking industry might have taken off like a rocket and left your fund with annual returns of 30 percent or more. Now, though, you believe that the glory days are gone and that banking is no longer the growth industry it was two years ago. Maybe it's a good time to sell the banking sector fund for a different sector or to move that money into something more conservative.

It could just be that you change your mind. The more time you spend investing in mutual funds, the more skilled you'll be. Years after choosing a fund, you might find later that you disagree with your initial choice. You aren't running for political office; it's okay to change your mind. Sell the old fund and move to one you think is a better choice.

When the Fund's Return Continually Lags Behind Its Peers

You can only lose money for so long before you begin to question the soundness of an investment. Even if you purchase a volatile fund and expect short-term losses, if they are too severe it might not be worth the ride. Fluctuations are inevitable, so how do you know when they indicate a time to sell?

By comparing your fund to its peers. It's important that you don't compare it to funds with different objectives or strategies. Parts of the market move into and out of favor at different times. Don't compare your fund that's operating in a currently unfavored part of the market with a fund that's operating in the market's current favorite. For example, it doesn't do any good to compare your retirement account in an S&P 500 index fund with your emergency reserve tucked away in a tax-free money market fund. They're birds of a different feather and don't fly the same breezes.

Compare your large company growth fund with other large company growth funds, your zero-coupon bond fund with other zero-coupon bond funds, and so on. If your fund's annual return is at the bottom of the heap for too long, dump it for one that's consistently at the top.

How long is too long to spend at the bottom of the heap? I've heard everything from three months to six years. In my opinion, the answer is two to three years. Anything less than two doesn't give the market time to overcome random chance. Much longer than three years leaves too much time for missed opportunity. If your fund can't fight its way to the top third of its class in at least one out of the three years, it's time to move your money to one that can.

When the Fund Doesn't Do What You Thought It Would

Every now and then you'll buy a fund that looked like a certain type of fund in the prospectus, but turns out to be something different. Prospectuses often contain a great deal of flexibility in fine print regarding what the fund manager can do. For example, if the flexibility is substantial enough, your growth fund manager could change to an income strategy by purchasing more bonds than stocks if he thinks the stock market is destined for a fall. In the fund's semiannual report, you might notice that he sold a lot of stock and bought a lot of bonds. Maybe his move would save money if the market falls.

Then again, maybe you resent the change. It's your money. If you had wanted to put it into a fund that purchased bonds, you would have. You purchased the growth fund expecting it to buy growth stocks. When it changed strategies, it could be a signal to you that your money would be better served elsewhere.

When the Fund Manager Leaves

A mutual fund is only as good as its manager. When you purchase a fund because of its past performance, what you're really purchasing is the ability of the fund manager to pick investments better than his or her peers. If that manager leaves, the fund's continued success might be jeopardized.

Industry research confirms this commonsense notion. Various studies show that funds placing in the top ranks of their categories usually suffer from a management change, while funds placing in the bottom ranks of their categories usually benefit from a management change. Of course, this isn't always the case. Some funds are managed by teams and adapt well when one member of the team departs. Other funds, such as Fidelity Magellan, have switched from one outstanding manager to the next without problem. All in all, however, funds that make smooth transitions from one manager to the next are the exception.

Even if you don't sell a fund whose manager is changing, you should at least pay extra attention to its performance. Watch for sudden changes and have a backup fund in mind should you decide it's time to switch.

Also, don't assume that because the fund is part of a large fund company, the company's reputation is enough to keep the fund afloat. It's the individual fund that matters and one of the most important components of the individual fund is its manager. Remember when you were a kid that it was the teacher, not the school, who made a class worthwhile? It's the same way with mutual funds. The manager, not the fund company, makes the fund worthwhile.

A new manager makes past performance virtually irrelevant. Sure, the fund's investment philosophy and general strategy remain intact, but the investment-picking skill begins at square one with no track record whatsoever in your fund. Your investment is suddenly entering a new fund and, since that's the case, you might as well look among the fund's peers to see if there's a more attractive choice. If you're entering into a new fund anyway, you should make it the best one. You might conclude that there are no better choices, but don't do so out of laziness. Research is time well spent.

Sometimes a new fund manager is a good thing. If your fund has been doing poorly and along comes a new manager, hopefully the performance will improve. Also, while it's true that the new manager does not have a track record in the fund, he or she probably has a track record of some sort. Did the new manager pick investments for a fund similar to the one he or she is taking over? If so, how did the previous fund do? The right answers to these questions can be a green light for investors. For example, few would squawk if they learned that Peter Lynch and Warren Buffet were taking over their mutual fund. Most likely the fund would triple its size as news got out that two of the finest investors of our time were teaming up to manage an existing fund.

The bottom line is that you should watch a fund closely if its manager changes. In all likelihood, its performance will change too. Be prepared to sell if things get ugly.

How to Sell a Fund

Getting your money out of a mutual fund is called redeeming your shares. When you redeem a share of a mutual fund, you sell it back to the fund company for the current NAV. You can redeem all or a portion of your shares, depending on how much money you want to take out of the fund.

The major fund companies allow you to call their toll-free numbers to request a redemption. Unfortunately, they mail a check the next day, so there's a lag between your request and the arrival of a check.

To solve this, you can establish quicker methods of redeeming shares. In money market accounts, for example, check-writing privileges are a common feature. In that case you can write a check from your money market fund exactly as you would do from your checking account.

Other methods of redemption are bank wire transfer and direct deposit. Both are faster at getting the money to you and, with direct deposit, the money is instantly credited to your bank account. You don't even need to wait in line to deposit it. The money just shows up in your account.

To learn about your fund company's redemption options, call its toll-free number and tell the representative what method you prefer. He or she will send necessary forms and set up your account.

5 Tracking Your Funds

An important part of investing in mutual funds is tracking their performance. If you choose your funds wisely, chances are good that you won't have to change direction later. But just in case, you should keep tabs on each fund. This chapter explains three ways to do so: mailings from the fund, publications, and resources for serious investors.

Mailings from the Fund

From time to time, mutual fund companies mail their investors newsletters and updates on fund performance.

I suggest you keep these and other records pertaining to your fund in a file with the fund's name on top. That way when it's time to call the mutual fund, you'll have all necessary information in the same place.

Account Statements

Mutual fund companies send out statements similar to the kind you receive from your bank. The statement provides a summary of transactions that you've made such as purchasing new shares in the fund or selling what you owned. Year-end statements also report capital gains and losses that the fund has posted to your account, which you'll need for your tax returns. You'll read more about taxes on page 109. I'm sure you can't wait.

Earlier I discussed reinvesting your distributions. The fund statement is where you'll be able to see the wisdom of your decision. Along with your regular transactions, the fund lists reinvestments. You can see the amount your total worth grew with each reinvestment. You'll also see the investments that happened automatically if you established an automatic investment plan.

Some funds send statements of confirmation every time you send new money, regardless of whether the money came from an automatic investment or from your checkbook. You don't need to save confirmation statements unless there appears to be a discrepancy. Just check them to see that the fund received the proper amount of money and invested it in the right place. All information contained on confirmation statements is reflected in regular summary statements.

Many investors find that the best way to keep track of statements is in a three-ring binder. Some fund companies even prepunch the holes in important statements indicating which material should be saved.

Literature

In addition to account statements, some funds send material like newsletters, performance updates, or advertisements. The information is usually good to have, and you should take a moment to look it over.

Fund Literature Provides Helpful Information

Some of the larger fund companies have material prepared by outside organizations like Standard and Poor's. The information is sometimes more relevant than you'll find in a magazine. Your fund expenses are paying for the mailings, so you should take advantage of them.

Fund newsletters are a good way to keep tabs on what's happening at your fund company. They announce new funds, discuss strategies in current funds, and showcase fund managers who provide their predictions on the market. Flip through the issues you receive, and if one contains information important to your investments, stick it in your folder or three-ring binder.

Don't confuse fund newsletters with subscription newsletters. Subscription newsletters try to make predictions on the market and suggest which funds to buy and sell. They also charge a lot. You'll read more about subscription newsletters in the textbox on page 101.

Publications

It's a good idea to continue examining unbiased information about your funds after you own them. It helped in your research, and it will help throughout the life of your investment.

Newspaper Listings

The financial pages of major newspapers carry daily mutual fund prices. You can see the NAV of your funds at any time. Let's say you own shares in the Pretend Family Fictional Fund and want to see how it's doing. Here's what you might find in the paper:

Pretend Family

Fictional Fund (r)	9.26 9.72 + .05
BuyMe Fund (p)	9.98 N.L. + .11
Another Fund	8.32 (8.74) –.22

Another Family

Fictional Fund r	9.26 9.72 + .05
BuyMe Fund p	9.98 N.L. + .11
Another Fund	8.32 8.74–.22

(r): Tells you that the fund charges a CDSC or a redemption fee.

(p): Tells you that the fund has a 12b-1 plan.

(8.74): This number is the buying price per share. The first number is the NAV. If the fund lists a second number, that means it has an up-front load. If you already own shares in the fund, you sell them at the first price. To buy new shares, you pay the second price.

Financial Listings Are Fun to Read During Bull Markets

Some newspapers abbreviate fund names, and others use different symbols. At the beginning of the mutual fund listings, most papers explain how to read the listings and provide a key to their own symbols.

Remember that well-researched funds don't need to be checked daily. You're not looking to "time" the market by hopping on a skyrocket and jumping off when it reaches the stratosphere. If you followed the advice in this guidebook, you own carefully selected funds that will provide the returns you expect in the time period appropriate for your goals. An annual price check is necessary, a quarterly one is a good idea, and monthly ones are about as detailed as you need to get.

Whenever you want the price, though, you'll find it in the financial pages.

Magazines

Once you get started in the investment world, it's smart to receive information about what's happening. Magazines are a great way to do so because they provide overviews of the market instead of detailed examinations. Mutual fund investors don't usually need to know details—fund managers do. Not knowing details doesn't mean sticking your head in the sand, however. It means letting someone else tend the finer points while you tend the big issues affecting you, like your goals and personal finances. It's important for you to read about economic trends, but not necessarily about what the CEO of a major corporation did with his stock options yesterday. Reading good magazines will make you an informed investor in the areas that matter to you most.

Among the many financial magazines available, I think four stand out from the crowd. I know this is controversial and that every title on the rack boasts a loyal readership, but these are my picks in order of preference:

1. *SmartMoney*

My Favorite Financial Magazine

Published by Dow Jones, which is the same company that publishes the *Wall Street Journal*, this magazine is one of the best all-around personal finance periodicals. It provides good coverage of the mutual fund industry but doesn't lose track of the economic environment in which funds operate. This is helpful to fund investors. Knowing what the market is doing, what the government has planned, and about economic trends are all necessary to understanding the behavior of funds. *SmartMoney* also includes helpful articles on other financial aspects of life such as choosing a phone company, buying a car, carrying insurance, and vacationing.

SmartMoney subscriptions are $24 a year and can be ordered at 800-444-4204.

2. *Worth*

A very close second on my list. For interesting articles *Worth* is hard to beat. Its balance of coverage between mutual funds, stocks, and bonds is great, and it also has an uncanny way of addressing topics that just happen to be on your mind. The magazine's subtitle is "financial intelligence" and that's exactly what its readers receive.

Worth subscriptions are $24 a year and can be ordered at 800-777-1851.

3. *Kiplinger's*

Kiplinger's has many of the same qualities as *SmartMoney*. It publishes some of the best mutual fund listings throughout the year with clear graphics and explanations. It isn't a "me too" publication, so you don't have to worry about reading hype. It provides articles of interest to everybody and keeps mutual funds in context.

Kiplinger's subscriptions are $20 a year and can be ordered at 800-544-0155.

4. *Mutual Funds*

This is a new player in the magazine market and the only publication devoted exclusively to mutual funds. It complements any of the three magazines above since they cover the broader economy while *Mutual Funds* covers fund issues specifically. The magazine's articles are excellent, and its inexpensive subscription rate is hard to pass up. You can also use your computer to view it on the World Wide Web for free. Its Web address is http://www.mfmag.com.

Mutual Funds charges $15 a year and can be ordered at 800-442-9000.

What's So Great About Subscription Newsletters?

In the investment world, everybody seems to have a favorite subscription newsletter—one they think finds the best mutual funds or has figured out a formula for timing stocks. These specialized publications are usually expensive, priced from $50 and up. Most fund newsletters fall into one of two categories: those that teach how to invest and those that tell when to buy, hold, or sell certain funds.

My favorite newsletters are the ones that teach and tell at the same time. It's nice to know when to buy and sell, but if you don't understand what's driving the recommendations, you'll never become a better investor. By reading informative articles and watching the model portfolios in these combination newsletters, you'll hone your skills and become your own best investment adviser. On that note, here are my favorite mutual fund newsletters:

- **"The Neatest Little FundLetter," $75. Surprise, surprise, guess who writes this one? I do! Each issue presents helpful articles written in the same style I use in this book. The newsletter features FundFolio, an exclusive system of nine model portfolios that chooses funds based on how much you invest and your time frame, and Kelly's Quicklist, my favorite funds grouped by category. To subscribe, call toll free 800-339-5671 or browse the Web at http://www.jasonkelly.com.**
- **"Morningstar Investor," $79. Provides insightful articles and data on 500 funds chosen by *Morningstar*'s editors. The company's reputation in the mutual fund industry is unparalleled. I like this**

newsletter a lot. To subscribe, call toll free 800-735-0700.

- **"Moneyletter," $152. Keeps tabs on the economy, summarizes market trends, and recommends funds in model portfolios. Also provides an investor hotline. To subscribe, call 508-881-2800.**
- **"The No-Load Fund Investor," $119. Reports industry news, tracks 800 funds, and recommends funds in model portfolios. A beefy data source for serious investors. To subscribe, call 914-693-7420.**

For a list of other titles, see *The Oxbridge Directory of Newsletters* at your library.

Radio and Television

Instead of listening to music while you drive, you can tune into a financial radio broadcast. National Public Radio (NPR) airs excellent information on mutual funds, U.S. and foreign stock markets, economic trends, and worldwide news. NPR regularly hosts financial experts who provide advice to listeners and sometimes offer informative literature by mail. To find a local radio station that broadcasts the program, call NPR at 202-414-3232.

Financial programs on your local television stations probably cover mutual funds from time to time. On cable, CNBC airs daily specials and occasional coverage of international investments. CNN offers investment information during its morning and evening business reports, and also airs a program called *MoneyLine.*

Resources for Serious Investors

Some investors monitor their mutual funds copiously. If you are one of them and would like to move beyond newspaper listings and standard investment magazines, you'll be interested in these additional resources.

Professional Publications

Professional publications will turn you into a mutual fund expert. Morningstar and Value Line provide you with enough information to study all night long. The Worth Portfolio Alert tracks your portfolio for you and faxes a summary on business days.

Morningstar

Morningstar has become a standard source of information for the mutual fund industry. Based in Chicago, the company supplies analysis to magazines for ranking purposes and helps investment professionals choose the right funds for their clients. If you followed my advice, you might have used its *Morningstar Mutual Funds* sourcebook in your initial fund research.

Morningstar Is for Investers Planning to Do Thorough Analysis

Morningstar offers a newsletter called "Morningstar Investor," the biweekly inserts for its sourcebook, a special sourcebook for no-load funds, and a software package. *Morningstar Mutual Funds* costs $395 for an annual subscription and offers a 3-month trial subscription for $55. None of Morningstar's information is cheap, but its reputation is second to none.

Unless you have a lot of money at stake and enjoy thoroughly analyzing your funds, it isn't necessary to deal directly with Morningstar. It made sense in your initial research, but not on a twice-monthly basis for tracking your funds. Perhaps for your annual fund checkups you could make a trip back to the library and take advantage of *Morningstar Mutual Funds* again.

For regular information I recommend the investment magazines. They'll give you Morningstar information in fund rankings and articles, and they're much more affordable.

For more information about Morningstar products, call 800-735-0700.

Value Line

An alternative to Morningstar, Value Line also supplies mutual fund analysis to professional investors. It is not as often cited in magazines or advertising as Morningstar, but Value Line is quickly catching on among individuals who want more than a consumer investment magazine but can't afford Morningstar.

The Value Line Mutual Fund Survey covers more funds than *Morningstar Mutual Funds*, costs less, and comes with some nice fringe benefits. For the $295 annual subscription price you also receive a newsletter and an investment booklet.

The same caveats you read about Morningstar's products apply to Value Line's. I don't see any reason why investors can't get by on a good magazine as long as their funds were well researched and they track them regularly.

For more information about Value Line products, call 800-284-7607.

Worth Portfolio Alert

A Customized Fax Service

This is a customized fax service offered by *Worth* magazine. You tell Portfolio Alert what investments you own, and it tracks them for you. Every morning or evening on weekdays you receive a fax that shows the value of your investments and summarizes news that affects them. Portfolio Alert charges $195 per year and offers a free one-week trial.

Unless you own very volatile funds and plan to switch among them in an attempt to time the market—a practice I strongly discourage—these daily updates are more information than you need. Also, you can check daily prices in any major newspaper.

For more information about Portfolio Alert, call 800-717-2220 or fax your name and address to 800-841-5397.

Computer Software

If you have a personal computer, you might be interested in the two mutual fund databases in this section. Since software companies are constantly adding features and expanding to different platforms, call the numbers to find out if the software is compatible with your computer.

Computers Make Short Work of Mutual Fund Research

Your Mutual Fund Selector

Produced by Intuit, who also makes Quicken, the best-selling personal finance program, Your Mutual Fund Selector is a collection of information on 1,000 funds. The program conducts an interview with you to determine your financial status and tolerance for risk and then recommends a group of funds for your consideration.

The data is supplied by Morningstar. Each fund page includes such helpful figures as a performance graph, beta, R-squared, expense ratio, manager tenure, and the fund's toll-free number.

The program is available as part of Quicken Deluxe and Quicken Financial Planner. You're entitled to one free quarterly update disk that installs the latest fund information on your computer. You can subscribe to additional updates for a fee.

For information, contact Intuit at 800-624-6930. To order, call 800-325-1538.

Mutual Fund Expert

This program is produced by Steele Systems, Inc., and tracks thousands of funds. Instead of conducting an interview with you, Mutual Fund Expert allows you to enter desired values in each of the program's data fields, and it finds the funds matching your criteria.

For example, you could tell the program that you want funds that have expense ratios less than 1 percent, 10-year returns greater than 15 percent, no loads, and low betas. Mutual Fund Expert would return a list of funds that match those criteria. Once you have the list, you can sort it by whichever measurement you find most important, like total return. Then you'd have a list of the funds that match your criteria ordered from the highest total return to the lowest. It's a real time saver when you're doing research.

Mutual Fund Expert costs $50 and is available from Steele Systems, Inc., by calling 800-237-8400.

Online Services

With a Modem You Can Use Online Services

This field is growing in popularity. With computers arriving in more homes every day, electronic information is becoming a prime source of knowledge. All you need is a computer, a modem, and special software for the service you choose. You can use an online service to check the value of your funds.

Commercial Services

For a monthly fee you can use your computer to dial into an online collection of information. Once connected, you choose from a number of different categories like news, sports, and investing. It's a good place to read notes that other investors post and to get mutual fund information. The following companies are three of my favorites for mutual fund information.

America Online America Online has a dedicated mutual fund section that contains *Morningstar Mutual Funds.* You can search on funds in the Morningstar database and download pages to your computer for printing. America Online charges $9.95 a month, which gets you 10 hours of usage the first month and 5 hours each subsequent month. Additional time is billed at $2.95 per hour. To order or for more information, contact America Online at 800-827-6364.

CompuServe Billing itself as "the information service you won't outgrow," CompuServe offers a variety of investment information. For mutual fund investors the best service is FundWatch Online by *Money* magazine. FundWatch allows you to screen funds by several different categories like their expense ratios or performance ratings. CompuServe charges $39.95 for a membership kit, which gives you one month of unlimited use. Subsequent months cost $9.95 for basic consumer databases and news, and $4.80 per hour for most other services. To order or for more information, contact CompuServe at 800-848-8199.

Dow Jones Market Monitor If you want an online service that only targets investing, the Dow Jones Market Monitor is for you. It doesn't give information on vacations, sports, or movie reviews like America Online and CompuServe, but it provides much more investment information. For example, the Market Monitor carries complete articles from the *Wall Street Journal* and *Barron's,* late-breaking stories from the Dow Jones news wires, information on nearly 5,000 mutual funds, and reports on insider trading activity. It's a truly comprehensive service, and is probably overkill if your only investments are mutual funds. Still,

among investment information services this one is tops. The Dow Jones Market Monitor charges $29.95 a month, which gives you 8 hours of usage. Additional time is billed at $3.60 per hour. To order or for more information, call Dow Jones at 800-815-5100.

The World Wide Web

The World Wide Web is a point-and-click multimedia interface that makes getting information from the internet easy. The Web is a collection of pages containing information such as pictures, charts, texts, and buttons that point you to other pages. Unlike commercial online services, the Web is free to everybody. You need a modem and a Web browser to view the pages. For more information about accessing the Web, call your local software store. *Mutual Funds* magazine, which I recommend to you on page 100, appears on the Web at http://www.mfmag.com. Here are some other helpful Web sites:

Jason Kelly This is my Web site. It answers frequently asked questions, profiles select funds from my Quicklist, features how-to columns, contains information about my newsletter, and provides links to other sites helpful to mutual fund investors. You can also see a schedule of upcoming seminars and send me a note if you'd like. My address is http://www.jasonkelly.com.

You Learn a Lot on the Web!

The Mutual Funds Home Page This is an excellent site for beginners and seasoned pros alike. A section called Funds 101 teaches newcomers how to invest. It features how-to columns and book excerpts. Another section called Expert's Corner showcases articles by guest experts from the fund industry. The articles cover everything from buy-and-hold strategies to the direction of the economy. The site also offers news, price quotes, and a free online newsletter. The Mutual Funds Home Page's address is http://www.brill.com.

Networth This a great research tool! It shows details like fund prospectuses and performance figures, but also provides services like newsletter subscriptions and promotional materials. A banner at the top of its main menu page shows the S&P 500 return, updated every 15 minutes. You can access Morningstar's database and get price quotes from Standard & Poor's. You can even use discussion forums to communicate with fund experts. Each week features a different panel of experts. Networth's address is http://www.networth.galt.com.

Search Tools The Web is constantly changing. To conduct your own searches and find online sites that appeal to you, try these search tools.

AltaVista Run by Digital Equipment Corporation, AltaVista gives you access to the largest Web index. It finds new sites every day and is the fastest Web-search engine I've used. AltaVista's address is http://www.altavista.digital.com.

Excite Excite uses a concept-based search to keep results related to what you're looking for. It ranks findings by how relevant it thinks they are to your search. The accuracy of the rankings varies, but is fairly good. Excite's address is http://www.excite.com.

Lycos If you want everything including the kitchen sink, Lycos is for you. Searches on this site return tons of places to visit. Use Lycos to scour every nook and cranny of the online world. Lycos' address is http://www.lycos.com.

Yahoo Yahoo was one of the first Web directories and is still popular today. Its searches are getting smarter all the time. Enter "mutual funds" on the opening search line, and you'll get just about everything you need. Yahoo's address is http://www.yahoo.com.

6 Other Investment Considerations

This chapter covers tax issues related to investing in mutual funds, special retirement accounts available to you, and ways to consolidate your investments.

Taxes

This is the topic that everybody hates but nobody can ignore. Taxes are probably the most tedious part of mutual fund investing. Then too, they're probably the most tedious part of life in general.

I don't provide you with exhaustive details regarding the tax law, but this section covers the basics of mutual fund tax considerations.

Capital Gains and Losses

A capital gain is the profit you receive when you sell an investment for more than what you paid. A capital loss is the amount of money you lose when you sell an investment for less than what you paid. Capital gains are taxable income and must be reported to the IRS on your annual tax return. Capital losses are deducted from your annual income and are also reported on your tax return.

Capital gains and losses are classified as short-term for

Short-term: Investments Held Less Than 12 Months

Long-term: Investments Held More Than 12 Months

investments held 12 months or less, or long-term for investments held more than 12 months. This is important to know because short-term gains are taxed at your normal rate while long-term gains have a maximum tax of 28 percent.

With mutual funds there are two ways to realize capital gains and losses. The first is to receive distributions from the fund. The second is for you to sell your mutual fund shares. Each way is explained below.

Capital Gain Distributions

When your mutual fund sells its stocks or bonds at a profit, it passes the profit to you. Even though you didn't sell the investments yourself, you have realized a capital gain. However, if your fund sells an investment at a loss, shareholders do not realize a capital loss. Instead the loss is deducted from the mutual fund's NAV. To avoid taxing the money twice, your mutual fund company does not pay tax on the capital gains before distributing them to you. The money you receive is called a capital gain distribution and is reported to the IRS on Schedule D of your annual tax return.

Since you didn't actually create the distribution income, it is up to the fund to determine whether distributions are short- or long-term. It does so based on how long it held its investments and reports the results to you on a year-end form called a 1099-DIV.

To minimize capital gain distributions for tax purposes, choose funds with low portfolio turnover rates. Remember from page 77 that portfolio turnover rate tells you how frequently the fund manager is buying and selling securities. If the manager constantly turns over the fund's portfolio, there is a greater chance of incurring a capital gain.

Selling Fund Shares

When you sell your mutual fund shares, you realize a capital gain or loss just as the fund does when it sells individual stocks that it owns. The capital gain is determined by subtracting the price you paid for the shares from your selling price. Of course, if the number is negative, then you have realized a capital loss and will be able to deduct it from your annual income.

When figuring out what price you paid for your shares, it's more complicated than just looking back at the NAV on the day you purchased them. For shares held longer than 90 days you must also add any brokerage expenses you paid when purchasing the funds. Then the resulting number is divided by the total number of shares purchased. The final price is called your cost basis, and it is what you subtract from the selling price of your shares.

Buying Through a Broker Makes Taxes Difficult

Good News: You Don't Have to Suffer Through It

For example, say you bought 100 shares of a no-load fund with a NAV of $15 through a broker who charged a $100 commission. The price of your investment is 100 shares × $15 or $1,500. Add the $100 commission and you get a total of $1,600. Divide $1,600 by the 100 shares and your price per share is actually $16. So if you sell the shares at a $20 NAV, your capital gain is only $4 per share—not $5. There is an exception to this rule. If you sell your shares within 90 days of purchasing them and reinvest the money in the same fund or another fund at the same company without paying a new sales charge, the IRS will not allow you to factor brokerage commissions into the cost of your original shares.

Since I have shown you how to purchase no-load funds without a broker, your cost basis is simply the NAV that you paid when you invested. This is a major advantage to being an independent investor. Not only do you save money by not paying a broker to begin with, you also save yourself the hassle of computing cost basis at tax time.

If you have dividends automatically reinvested in a mutual fund, they will purchase additional shares at a price that is probably different from what you paid for your initial investment. That means that when you sell shares, some will earn more profit than others. Put another way, your average cost per share changes when you buy additional shares at different prices.

There are two methods of determining the purchase price of the shares you sell. The first is simply to average all of the purchase prices together and use the average price for all shares. The second is to keep track of exactly the amount you paid for each share and specify which shares you want to sell. Most investors prefer the average-cost method over the specific-price method.

The year-end statement from your fund reports these capital gains, which you'll need to know for your tax returns. Plus, fund companies send you 1099-B forms if you sold or exchanged shares during the year. The forms compute tax information for you.

Ordinary Dividends

When your mutual fund earns interest from its cash or bonds, or its stocks pay dividends, you receive a dividend payment from the mutual fund. This dividend isn't a capital gain because the fund didn't sell any investments; it simply earned money on the investments it already held. The money you receive is called an ordinary dividend and is reported to the IRS on Schedule B of your annual tax return.

Retirement Savings Can Be Tax-deferred

As with capital gains, you can have ordinary dividends reinvested automatically in the fund. Since ordinary dividends are considered short-term income, they are taxed at your regular rate.

At the end of each year, fund companies send you 1099-DIV forms that report all of your ordinary dividend and capital gain distributions.

An Example of How All This Works

Let's say you invested $1,000 in a growth stock fund with a $10 NAV. Your money purchased a total of 100 shares. Six months later, the fund reinvested an ordinary dividend of $.75 per share and a capital gain distribution of $.95 per share. During the six months between your initial investment and the two reinvestments, the fund's NAV dropped to $9. Here's what happened:

- The ordinary dividend reinvestment purchased the following:

  1) .75 dividend × 100 shares = $75 total dividend
  2) $75 total dividend ÷ $9 NAV = **8.33 shares purchased**

- The capital gain distribution reinvestment purchased the following:

  1) .95 dividend × 100 shares = $95 total dividend
  2) $95 total dividend ÷ $9 NAV = **10.55 shares purchased**

- Add the two purchases to determine the total number of new shares:

  1) 8.33 ordinary dividend shares purchased
  2) 10.55 capital gain shares purchased
  3) 8.33 + 10.55 = **18.88 total new shares purchased**

Let's say three months later the fund's NAV rises to $11. You decide to make a quick profit by selling all 118.88 of your shares. Here's the outcome using the average-cost method to determine purchasing price:

"The nation should have a tax system which looks like someone designed it on purpose."
—William Simon

- Your cost basis (the total amount of money you paid for all your shares) is:

  1) $1,000 initial investment
  2) $75 ordinary dividend reinvestment
  3) $95 capital gain reinvestment
  4) $1,000 + $75 + $95 = **$1,170 cost basis**

- Your tax basis (the average price you paid per share) is:

  $1,170 cost basis ÷ 118.88 shares = **$9.84 tax basis**

- Your capital gain is:

  1) 118.88 shares × $11 current NAV = $1,307.68 proceeds
  2) 118.88 shares × $9.84 tax basis = $1,169.78 tax cost
  3) $1,307.68 proceeds – $1,169.78 tax cost = **$137.90 capital gain**

Since you held the mutual fund for nine months, you would report a $137.90 short-term capital gain on your annual tax return.

Any of the major tax books such as those from J. K. Lasser, H&R Block, *Consumer Reports*, or *Money* will explain the full tax situation as it applies to mutual fund investors. Contact your local bookstore for pricing and availability.

This Tax Stuff Is Lots of Fun. Can You Tell Me More?

Unfortunately, yes. I know how boring tax information can be, but I don't make the laws. The following are several items to keep in mind when thinking about taxes and your mutual funds:

- **After paying the tax on distributions, you can add it to your future cost basis. That way you won't be taxed twice on the same money. For example, say you invest $1,000 in a fund in 1995, pay $10 in taxes during 1995, and sell everything for $2,000 in 1996. Your capital gain is not $1,000 ($2,000 proceeds – $1,000 tax cost). It's $990 because you add the $10 tax to your tax cost: $2,000 – $1,010 = $990 capital gain.**
- **There's neither a capital gain nor a capital loss when you sell shares in a money market fund. That's because money market funds maintain a constant $1 NAV. You pay tax on the fund's distributions, however.**
- **If you switch money from one fund to another, it is considered selling the first and purchasing the second for tax purposes. Thus, any capital gain on the sale must be reported as though you received a check.**
- **Distributions that are automatically reinvested must still be reported as income.**
- **Tax-free distributions must be reported to the IRS every year even though you do not owe tax on them.**
- **"Nothing can be said to be certain, except death and taxes."—*Benjamin Franklin***

Retirement

Because retirement money is necessary in everybody's life, the government has established tax-deferred methods of investing for retirement. The money placed in retirement accounts can't be touched until a certain date but compounds tax-free until then. Upon retirement, withdrawals are taxed at the recipient's normal rate. Retirement accounts are also called "qualified plans" because of their tax-deferred status.

Since retirement is a long-term goal, most retirement money should be invested aggressively. Remember that stocks have outperformed both bonds and the money market over time. That means that if retirement is more than 11 years away, you should allocate the majority of your retirement money to stock funds. Also, consider allocating a portion of your retirement money to international funds. To read about allocating your money, see page 24.

An important point to keep in mind as you invest for retirement is that retirement plans are tax-deferred. Therefore it doesn't make sense to place retirement money in a fund that is tax-free, such as a municipal bond fund. You don't pay capital gains tax or ordinary income tax on *any* money held in a retirement account. All your retirement account money should be invested in funds that are not tax-free. Otherwise you'll receive lower tax-free yields.

Retirement planning involves five stages. They are:

1. Deciding what it will cost you to live during retirement.
2. Totaling the income you will receive from Social Security and company pension plans.
3. Calculating the amount you must save to cover the difference between your retirement costs and the income from Social Security and pension plans.
4. Choosing an allocation for your retirement savings.
5. Maintaining an investment schedule that will produce the needed savings.

To help you navigate these five stages, fund companies have designed retirement kits. I recommend that you contact fund companies that interest you and request that they send you a kit. They will do so free of charge with the hope that you'll choose them for your retirement account. These three companies have outstanding kits:

Free Information!

- Twentieth Century (800-345-2021) has a 26-page booklet called "Planning Today, Enjoying Tomorrow" which is one of the best step-by-step retirement guides I've seen. It even comes with a calculation wheel for anticipated rates of return and is filled with helpful worksheets.
- T. Rowe Price (800-541-5940) provides its Retirement Planning Kit, which is quite comprehensive. Its 90-line workbook leaves nothing to chance. The company also provides a kit for those who are already retired called the Retirees Financial Guide, which includes detailed worksheets and a request for benefits form that is addressed to the Social Security Administration.
- Fidelity Investment (800-544-8888) publishes a 16-page booklet called "A Common Sense Guide to Planning for Retirement." It presents the five retirement planning stages clearly and also comes with simple worksheets.

The following are three of the most popular retirement options, all of which are available to mutual fund investors.

Company-Sponsored Plans

Many companies offer plans that allow employees to deduct money automatically from their paychecks and place it in tax-sheltered investments. The deduction occurs before taxes are taken out, which reduces the employee's taxable income.

The most popular company-sponsored plans are the 401(k) for employees of regular businesses and corporations, and the 403(b) for employees of tax-exempt businesses.

In addition to saving money on taxes, participants in these

plans can also take advantage of matching contributions from their employers. Often, companies add between 25 and 100 percent of what the employee contributes. While not all companies make matching contributions, many see it as a good way to promote retirement savings and improve employee morale.

Sail Away on a Company Plan

The rewards of company-sponsored plans are great. Consider this: if you earn $30,000 a year and contribute 10 percent of your paycheck toward a 401(k), you'll set aside $3,000 annually. Since that $3,000 is not taxed, you save 28 percent of it or $840 just by avoiding tax. If your company matches 30 percent of your savings, that adds another $900 to your annual contribution. The final result is that you socked away a tidy $3,900 by only spending $2,160 (your $3,000 contribution minus the $840 you would have paid in tax). Plus, the money will grow tax-deferred until your retirement.

Saving Now Is Rewarding Later

Companies that offer retirement plans usually allow employees to choose from a limited selection of stock, bond, or money market mutual funds. Some companies manage the funds themselves while others hire a fund company to oversee the investments.

Some company plans allow employees to borrow money from their own retirement plan and pay it back to themselves. This is a great way to borrow money because employees are earning the interest for themselves. How would you like to buy your next car by borrowing the money from your own investment account? It's possible with many company-sponsored plans.

Call your employee-benefits counselor to learn what plans are available to you. If you are provided with a company-sponsored retirement plan, I strongly encourage you to take advantage of it.

Individual Retirement Accounts

The Individual Retirement Account (IRA) is designed for do-it-yourselfers. If you are younger than 70½, you may set aside up to $2,000 a year to grow tax-deferred in any investment you choose. If your spouse doesn't work, you may contribute $2,250 per year. The amount is deducted from your earned income and is therefore not taxed.

However, if you already contribute to a company-sponsored plan, the amount that you are able to deduct decreases. Since the deduction is determined by a number of factors, I suggest that you contact a tax preparer or annual tax handbook for the deduction available to you. Even if you can't deduct your IRA contribution, it's still a prudent retirement choice because the money grows tax-deferred.

You may begin withdrawing money from your IRA when you turn 59½. If you withdraw sooner, the money is taxed 10 percent plus your normal rate. So if you're in the 28 percent tax bracket and withdraw early, you'll lose a whopping 38 percent of your money. Upon reaching age 70½, you must begin withdrawing from your IRA. A popular strategy is to establish automatic monthly withdrawals that your mutual fund company sends to you, just like a paycheck. Even better, the monthly withdrawals can be deposited directly into one of your bank accounts.

An Individual Investor

The benefit of an IRA over a company-sponsored plan is that the entire investment market is available for your money, instead of the limited selection of company-sponsored mutual funds. The drawback is that nobody will match your contributions to an IRA. As its name implies, it is truly an "individual" retirement account.

Mutual fund companies have special IRA accounts that they will be happy to establish for you. They have forms just for IRA investors and will often waive loads on certain funds to encourage people to save for retirement. Call the company's toll-free number to request an IRA application if you are interested.

Self-employed Plans

If you are self-employed, even on a part-time basis, you may contribute money to a retirement account and have it grow tax-deferred. Your business must fund the plan, and if you have employees they must benefit equally from it along with you.

If you're a freelancer or moonlighter, however, you probably don't have employees. These plans can make retirement very comfortable.

There are two popular self-employed plans that I explain here, each of which resembles a company-sponsored plan more than an IRA.

Simplified Employee Pension—Individual Retirement Account

The Simplified Employee Pension—Individual Retirement Account (SEP-IRA) is the easiest retirement program for small business owners. It allows contributions of up to 13.04 percent of self-employment income, but not more than $22,500 annually. If you classify yourself as an employee of your business, the contribution may be up to 15 percent of your compensation, but not more than $30,000 annually. In addition, business owners and employees may still contribute the $2,000 yearly amount toward their regular IRA.

A Good Retirement Plan Has Its Benefits

The SEP-IRA is easy to establish and is discretionary, meaning that you can choose how much to contribute on a year-to-year basis. There is almost no paperwork involved. SEP-IRAs can be started anytime up to the filing deadline (usually April 15) for the tax year in which contributions will be claimed. So you could establish a SEP-IRA for 1996 anytime on or before April 15, 1997.

Keogh

A Keogh plan is much more complicated than a SEP-IRA. It's difficult to establish, has many variations, and requires detailed records for the IRS and the Department of Labor. Its main advantages are that it allows you to set aside more money each year and that it permits vesting schedules, which are varying rights to retirement money based on an employee's years of service. For most small business owners, the SEP-IRA is a better choice.

In most Keogh implementations, you may contribute up to 20 percent of your self-employment income but not more than

$30,000 per year. If you classify yourself as an employee of your business, the contribution may be up to 25 percent of your compensation but still not more than $30,000 per year. If you are older than 45 and make a lot of money, you may contribute more than the $30,000. The calculations for the actual amount are mind-numbing and generally require an accountant.

As you've probably gathered by now, Keoghs are best left to larger businesses unless vesting and higher contributions are needed. A Keogh plan must be started by the end of the tax year in which contributions will be claimed.

Consolidating Your Investments

Given the abundance of mutual funds available, it should come as no surprise that investors usually own several at once and switch from one to another occasionally. If your research turns up five funds that fit your goals like the ocean does the sea floor, you might be in for some paper chasing. You can imagine that receiving five different statements, calling five different toll-free numbers, and sending checks to five different addresses gets tiresome. You might reason that if those five funds are right for you, then it's worth it. But wouldn't it be nice if there was an easier way?

Sure, it would, and luckily you have two options. The first is to buy all your funds from the same fund family, and the second is to combine funds from different families using a discount broker. Each way is explained below.

Fund Families

A fund family is the total group of funds managed by the same company. The family usually covers all three basic objectives of growth, income, and stability. The two biggest mutual fund companies are Fidelity Investments and The Vanguard Group, each of whom offers hundreds of funds in their family. Other companies with large families include Invesco, Janus, Scudder, T. Rowe Price, and Twentieth Century.

The advantage of owning funds within a single family is that by calling one phone number you can buy or sell shares in any of your funds. You can also easily move money out of a stock fund and into a money market fund if you suddenly feel that stock prices are going to fall. I don't recommend timing the market like that, but there are times when you'll want to adjust your allocation by moving money from one fund to another. The convenience of a single point of contact can be great.

Owning Funds in the Same Family Is Convenient

You'll also receive a single statement detailing all of your mutual fund activity with that same company. This eases the burden on your record-keeping skills.

Discount Brokers

The obvious drawback to fund families is that one company might not own all the funds that fit your goals. Fidelity might have a couple, Janus another one, and a small fund company in Seattle a third. There's still a way to consolidate your investments in these different funds. It's called a discount broker.

Discount brokers dazzled the investment world by offering low brokerage commissions to investors buying individual stocks and bonds. People who didn't require advice on which stocks to buy opted for a cheaper commission instead. When mutual funds took the investment world by storm, discount brokers began offering them as well with cheap transaction costs.

Today several discount brokers offer mutual funds with *no* transaction costs. In other words, you can buy and sell funds from different companies through the same place without paying any more than you'd pay by purchasing from the fund companies themselves. Discount brokers are turning the entire mutual fund marketplace into one big family.

Discount Brokers Have It All

An added benefit to buying your funds through a discount broker is that if you ever decide to purchase an individual stock or bond, you can do so through the same place that handles your mutual fund investments.

In my opinion, the following are the three best discount brokers for mutual fund investors. Each offers excellent 24-hour phone service, hundreds of transaction-free funds, and a consolidated statement detailing all of your investment activity.

Charles Schwab & Company

Schwab pioneered the transaction-free fund idea and has remained at the forefront of this trend ever since. Schwab's One-Source offers more than 500 funds from first-rate companies like Invesco, Janus, and Twentieth Century. OneSource investors also benefit from Schwab's Mutual Fund Select List, which summarizes the best-performing funds every quarter, FundMap mutual fund selection software, and individual fund reports from Morningstar.

To receive more information about Schwab OneSource, call 800-266-5623.

Fidelity Investments

Fidelity's FundsNetwork offers over 400 funds, including its own funds. Offering its own funds is an important benefit because some of the best-performing funds are managed by Fidelity. The FundsNetwork includes funds from other companies like Berger, Heartland, PBHG, and Strong.

To receive more information about the FundsNetwork, call 800-544-8666.

Jack White & Company

Rated the best overall discount broker in America by *Smart-Money,* Jack White & Company offers more transaction-free funds than anybody else, over 800 at last count. However, the company's NoFee Network doesn't offer as many high-quality funds as Fidelity or Schwab. You will find a few companies that might be appropriate for you such as Benham, Crabbe Huson, and Warburg Pincus, but most of the blue-ribbon companies are notably absent.

To receive more information from Jack White & Company, call 800-233-3411.

Used rightly, money allows us to live, eat, drink, protect ourselves, help our families and friends, maintain our health, accomplish certain aims. This it does by reconciling external conflicts, by allowing relationships and exchanges to exist between elements that are not yet in relationship. It can be an instrument of love, hate, challenge, tenderness—all the normal feelings of a normal human being.

But used wrongly, money prevents relationship, prevents exchange between certain essential elements of the whole life. As a drug, money can simply substitute an external reconciliation for an internal confrontation of forces. It can *solve problems* where what is needed is the *experiencing of questions.* Like technology—and money is a form of technology—money is good at solving problems; it is bad at opening questions. Like technology, money is used wrongly when it converts inner questions that should be lived into problems to be solved. Money fixes things, but not every difficulty in life should be fixed. There are some difficulties that need to be lived with and experienced more and more consciously. The alcoholic, through a certain diseased relationship between personal emotions and blind instinctual sensations, is prevented from experiencing the confrontation of basic forces within himself. Therefore, he cannot develop *will,* which is the name the great teachings have given to the interior third force in man that relates his two natures. The money addict suffers from the same fundamental pathology.

—Jacob Needleman, *Money and the Meaning of Life*

7 Helpful Tools

This chapter provides twenty fund company phone numbers to get you started, parting words from yours truly, and the two worksheets that you've referenced while reading this guidebook.

20 Great Fund Companies and Their Phone Numbers

Opposite is a list of 20 mutual fund companies that offer excellent funds. If your research leads you to a fund from a company on this list, you're doing fine. That's not to say these 20 are the only providers of good funds—they're not. But all are well respected in the industry and can help you establish your investment program.

Even if you haven't done any research yet, consider calling a few of these companies to ask if they have beginner's guides. Each company spends time developing materials for their investors because they recognize that informed customers are the best customers. If you decide to call the companies before doing research, tell them that you are new to investing and would like to receive an overview of their fund family and any helpful guides they offer.

As you call these or any other mutual fund companies, keep in mind that you should always examine each fund that interests you. Never assume that just because a company offers one outstanding fund, all of its offerings are going to be as good. Each fund has a different objective and probably a different manager.

Benham	Founders	Mutual	Scudder
800-472-3389	800-525-2440	800-553-3014	800-225-2470
Berger	Harbor	Neuberger/Berman	Strong
800-333-1001	800-422-1050	800-877-9700	800-368-1030
Crabbe Huson	Heartland	PBHG	Twentieth Century
800-541-9732	800-432-7856	800-433-0051	800-345-2021
Dreyfus	Invesco	T. Rowe Price	Vanguard
800-782-6620	800-525-8085	800-638-5660	800-635-1511
Fidelity	Janus	Safeco	Warburg Pincus
800-544-8888	800-525-8983	800-624-5711	800-257-5614

Parting Words

I hope this guidebook helps you enter the world of mutual funds. I think mutual funds are the best investment vehicle for most people and am pleased to show how they can be purchased without a broker. Remember:

- Regardless of how old you are, start your investment program now. It's always the right time to begin striving for your goals.

- Balance the amount of time to reach your goals with appropriate levels of risk. More time, more risk. Less time, less risk.
- Choose an allocation that fits your goals. Money market funds are good for short-term goals, income funds are good for medium-term goals, growth funds and international funds are good for long-term goals.
- Establish a regular investing schedule. When you make regular investments, you are dollar-cost averaging so your average price per share goes down. See if your funds offer automatic transfers from your bank account to your funds. If so, sign up to make investing easy and guarantee timely deposits.
- Monitor your allocation as time progresses. Differing returns among your growth, income, and money market funds can change the way your money is allocated among them. Rebalance your allocation if necessary.

- Check your mutual funds at least once a year. You might want to check them more often, but there's no need to monitor daily price changes. Let your fund managers handle details.

Let me know what you think of this guidebook. I tried to make it easy and fun. How did I do? Write to me care of this publisher and let me know! I'll consider your suggestions for the next edition. Maybe I'll even use you in an example.

Worksheets

The following pages contain two worksheets for you to use. You may photocopy them as needed for your personal investment program. If your friends try to borrow your guidebook to make photocopies for themselves, don't let them! After all, the real reason for investing is to boast the highest returns at holiday parties. So here's what you do:

1. Buy copies of this guidebook for all of your friends.
2. When the subject of investing comes up, tell them how well you're doing in mutual funds.
3. With a casual nod, hand them a copy of the guidebook and say, "Here's a little something to get you started. Call me if you have questions."

Just like that, you'll be a mutual fund guru.

Financial Goal Worksheet Information

This worksheet helps you define your goals. Note that it asks for you to calculate how much money you need to set aside assuming a 0 percent rate of return. That means that if your investments provide any return whatsoever, you will end up with more money than your goal requires.

However, the sheet does not take inflation into account. The money values you place on the sheet for your goals are in today's dollars. So if your goal is ten years away, you would actually need more of today's dollars to fund it.

These two factors taken together should balance out safely. Since inflation rarely goes above 5 percent and your mutual funds should provide an average return greater than that, you should reach your goals with more money than needed.

One other thing: This worksheet isn't comprehensive enough for retirement planning. If you're planning to invest for retirement, call the numbers listed on page 116 for free kits to help you. Everything you learned in this book about choosing the right funds still applies, but you need to include estimated rates of return, other sources of income, and inflation in your retirement calculations.

Why, you might ask, is it such a big deal to avoid planning retirement on this financial goal worksheet? Because the amount it tells you to save is too high and will discourage you. If your goal is to have $500,000 when you retire in 30 years, the worksheet tells you to save $1,389 per month. That's probably a bit more than you intend to sock away for your golden years. The amount is high because the worksheet assumes you'll get no return on your investments and have no other sources of income when you retire, such as Social Security and a company retirement plan. So do yourself a favor and call for one of the kits on page 116. Use the kit in conjunction with what you've learned in this guidebook.

I provide one example goal on the worksheet's first line. Pages 8 through 29 present information you need to consider when filling out this worksheet.

Mutual Fund Information Sheet Information

This worksheet helps you gather information when researching what mutual funds are right for your goals. The first line of the worksheet shows what the information for a terrible fund might look like, and the second line shows what an excellent fund might look like. They provide the extreme ends of the spectrum and help you see where your funds stack up. Take a copy of this sheet with you whenever you do research.

Pages 70 through 78 explain the measurements used on this worksheet.

Financial Goal Worksheet

What You Want	What It Will Cost	When You Want It	Annual Payment	Monthly Payment	Time Frame (years)	Acceptable Risk Level	Mutual Fund Allocation Percentages			
		Measured in Years	Cost Divided by Years	Annual Payment Divided by 12	Short-term: 0-5 Medium-term: 6-10 Long-term: Over 10	High, Medium, or Low	Stocks	Bonds	Money Market	International
[Example]Lexus	$45,000	5	$9,000	$750	Short-term	Low	25	40	35	0
1)										
2)										
3)										
4)										
5)										
6)										
7)										
8)										
9)										
10)										
11)										
12)										
13)										
14)										
15)										

Mutual Fund Information Sheet

Fund Name and Phone	3-Year	5-Year	10-Year	Relative Rating	Beta	Alpha	R-Squared	Standard Deviation	Initial Invest	Loads	Expense Ratio	Fund Size	Manager Since	Portfolio Turnover
[Example]Terrible	-18.77	-11.75	-10.5	Worst 25%	1.85	-1	0	20.5	$50,000	8.5% + redem	3.5%	$40 Billion	8:00 a.m.	500%
[Example]Excellent	35.25	30.35	25.45	Best 25%	1	10	50	5.5	$500	No-Load	0.85%	$100 Million	1980	20%
1)														
2)														
3)														
4)														
5)														
6)														
7)														
8)														
9)														
10)														
11)														
12)														
13)														
14)														
15)														
16)														
17)														
18)														

Glossary

Alpha
page 21

Takes the volatility information contained in beta and compares it to a fund's performance. The bigger the alpha, the better the fund has performed for its volatility. Use alpha to see if a fund's performance justifies the ups and downs of its price.

An alpha of 0 means that the fund performed as expected for a fund of its volatility. So if it was a fund with a beta of 1.25, then it did indeed outperform its market by 25 percent in up markets and underperform it by 25 percent in down markets. An alpha greater than 0 means that the fund has performed better than expected given its beta. A growth stock fund with an alpha greater than 0 either maintained losses closer to those of the S&P 500 during a market decline than its beta would suggest, or it returned more than it should have when the market rose. If the fund's beta was 1.25, maybe it beat the S&P 500 by 35 percent in a rising market instead of the 25 percent you would expect. Or, the fund might have only lost 5 percent more than the S&P 500 when the market fell.

Beta
page 20

Measures how volatile a fund has been compared to an appropriate index, usually the S&P 500. The bigger the beta, the more volatile the fund.

Each index has a beta of 1. If a fund has a beta of 1.25, then it is 25 percent more volatile than its market index. That means that if the market is rising upward, the fund should outperform the market by 25 percent. When the market falls, the fund should fall 25 percent lower too. A stock fund that fluctuates 5 percent less than the S&P 500 has a beta of .95.

Index
page 60

A bunch of stocks grouped together and monitored to see how they perform. This profile of a market segment provides a point of reference to gauge the relative performance of different investments. There are indexes that measure large companies, small companies, international markets, and bonds.

An investment index that almost everyone knows is the Dow Jones Industrial Average. It averages the performance of 30 blue chip stocks. The *Standard & Poor's 500 (S&P 500)* tracks the 500 U.S. companies with the highest stock value, giving weight to those that are biggest. It accounts for 80 percent of the New York Stock Exchange.

NAV
page 2

The "net asset value," which is the price of each mutual fund share. At the end of every day, the NAV is determined by dividing the value of a fund's investments by the number of shares sold. For example, if a fund owns $20 million worth of stocks, bonds, or money market instruments and investors hold 5 million shares of the fund, then the fund's NAV is $4. The fund arrives at $4 after dividing $20 million by 5 million.

R-squared
page 22

The amount of a fund's return that is based on the return of its index. While beta is usually measured against the S&P 500 stock index, R-squared is measured against an index that most closely tracks the kinds of investments that a given fund owns. An R-squared of 100 says that the fund merely duplicated its index while an R-squared of 25 says that only 25 percent of the fund's return is attributed to its index.

Standard Deviation
page 23

The percentage range that a fund's monthly return has "deviated" from its average return, or mean. The bigger the standard deviation, the more volatile the fund. While beta measures a fund's volatility relative to the S&P 500, standard deviation measures a fund's pure volatility. With beta, a fund is considered volatile if it is more volatile than the S&P 500. With standard deviation, a fund is considered volatile or stable based solely on the consistency of its own monthly returns.